How to be Self Confident

How to be Self Confident

Cross Land
BOOKS

HOW TO BE SELF CONFIDENT
ISBN 81-8408-134-0

First Edition : 2008

Published by :
INDIANA PUBLISHING HOUSE

For

Crossland BOOKS
2/13 Ansari Road, Darya Ganj,
New Delhi-110 002

Printed by:
Salasar Imaging Systems
C7/5, Lawrance Road Indl. Area, Delhi 110 035

Contents

Fears and Repressions...

To be at ease... Not to be shy! Millions of people dream of this! To be able to act unselfconsciously and no longer to feel that you are constantly being observed by others, to fear that you are being misjudged, to feel inferior and certain of failure... That wonderful dream again!

Shyness is always marked by a failure to come to terms with social, family and professional life. This is quite understandable, because a shy person is incapable of adapting himself to situations which, to him, seem dangerous.

Unfortunately, too many shy people think their affliction incurable. Sometimes they are even convinced of it. They may have been told so repeatedly. They have even been advised to make an effort of will to overcome it, which is absurd. If you tell an active person to walk, he will walk but if you say the same to an invalid he will only manage a few steps and then sit down again, breathless and discouraged.

Some other method has to be found. First of all, we must know what shyness is and whence it arises. We have to discover what has prevented a human being from developing normally. We have to find out precisely—in a person's education, religious upbringing, sex-life—what has caused the block. A shy person must learn to analyse himself and discover the causes of his shyness. If he knows what they are he will have plenty of ammunition to fight with. He will no longer find himself before this elusive enemy who grips him by the throat. He will know exactly what he is up against and be able to uproot it from his life.

All men aspire to a state of perfect balance and to be completely at ease with the world, because they realize that balance and ease are natural and normal.

But a shy person denies life because he is afraid. He denies it because he is plunged in a constant state of anxiety of his own making. He can do nothing but blame everything on to circumstances or bad luck.

Isn't it a pity to see the great potentialities of shy people go to waste in spite of all the intelligence they may have? Life goes on, but the shy ones stay put, petrified, finishing by believing their condition and their failures to be inevitable. They are driven to this conclusion, moreover, by the lack of understanding that they often encounter!

All men want peace of mind. All men seek happiness. The aim of this book is to point out the way to all those held fast in the bonds of shyness.

Chapter I

How Do You Feel?

You've put your best suit on and you've set off with the invitation in your pocket. Here you are at a cocktail party given by some people to whom you're little more than a name. You're holding a glass and you're leaning against some mantelpiece listening to someone gabbling something or other.

How do you feel? Yes, of course you're bored stiff. All right! But that's not what I'm getting at. Half-an-hour ago you entered the room. Some men dropped their voices and so did some of the women. Then you crossed the room. You stepped forward, greeted someone and were introduced. Someone handed you that boring drink. You found a good position for your elbow and pretended to listen.

Well, how do you feel? Your legs a bit rubbery ? Your stomach? None of that empty feeling produced by anxiety and stage-fright? How did you greet those people? Humbly Timidly? Sternly? Dryly? Amiably?

Just a minute! They're talking about you all of a sudden! They're turning round. They're going to speak to you. How do you feel, eh? Isn't that anxiety getting worse? Are you ready to speak to them without timidity or aggressiveness? Are you feeling quite normal? Or have you started cursing the fear that paralyses you every time people turn their attention on you?

Anyway, listen to the story of Mr. X. I call him Mr. X, and this can cover the millions of people like him...

From ease to fear

Mr. X. is at home and completely at his ease, everything's all right. No snags. He hums or whistles to himself, his voice is normal, his color good. He's not worried about anything. In any case, what is there for him to worry about?

But, watch Mr. X an hour later. He has left his house. He's walking along a busy street and now he's got to pass a café whose pavement tables are fully occupied. What does Mr. X do? Mr. X who had been strolling along, stooping a bit, suddenly straightens himself. His manner changes. His step becomes less confident. Then his manner changes again: he throws his shoulders back, his body stiffens, his chin juts out as if in defiance. His face takes on a hard, haughty expression. And Mr. X strides on, nose in the air, although the people in the café look at him without interest as he passes by.

That evening Mr. X pays a visit to some friends. He enters a room where there are already ten other people. Congratulations, hand-shakes and greetings. Once again, he feels people are looking at him. Hasn't he written an article that's created quite a stir? But he begins to lose his composure and a sort of vague fear emerges from deep within, and seizes him.

However, everything still seems to be all right. There are no alarming symptoms. Mr. X sits down, joins in the conversation, smiles, nods...

There's silence. The host's voice is heard; "Our friend, Mr. X, is going to say something about that article he wrote recently and which has created such a furore!"

Silence again. The host sits down, "Our friend...?" A thought flashes across the visitor's mind: "But is that me, this friend? I've got to... I've got to speak?... just like that? Without any warning? But I haven't prepared anything! I..."

He stands up. Fifteen or twenty pairs of eyes turn towards him with automatic precision. Men clear their throats and women smile. Everyone is waiting!

Mr. X is on his feet, rigid and scared. He realizes with terror that he has even forgotten the gist of his article. An article he knows very well because he wrote and rewrote it himself more than ten times!

He tries. He racks his brains. Nothing! A lump comes into his throat! Then, suddenly, a faint glimmer: the outline of his first paragraphs comes back to him. He begins. He speaks. He feels paralyzed. There's a mist in front of his eyes. He has the strange impression that his words vanish even while he is uttering them. He speaks mechanically. His lips are dry, his hands tremble—at first slightly, then violently. He stuffs his hands into his pockets to hide the trembling as it grows. His heart's thumping now! All those people are there, in a sort of swirling mist! The eyes of "the others" are still riveted on him. They are smiling! But for the speaker, there's no doubt about it—those smiles are ironical: they are mocking his awkwardness. He is sure he is gabbling, talking in little spurts about a lot of rubbish that's of no interest to anyone. Suddenly he feels wretched, humble, insignificant. But isn't he well-known, rich, good-looking? None of that counts any more! He feels his muscles contracting and his legs buckling under him. And when he runs his tongue over his lips, it is only to feel their terrible dryness...

He comes to the end. Has he spoken for a minute or for a century? He has no idea. He can't even remember what he's said. He felt all the time like an automaton plunged in a panic that froze him to the spot but at the same time made him want to run away as fast as he could.

It's over. The guests rise and congratulate him. Slowly he straightens himself; his whole body begins to unwind and exhaustion creeps over him. Furious with himself, he seethes at the "thing" that gets him every time he has to speak in public...

Why does it happen?

This man has had an attack of stage-fright. Who has not known these painful symptoms at some time or other in his life? How many people there must be who, in public, lose control of themselves as well as lose their opportunities!

What are they afraid of? *Why* are they afraid? Do they suffer from these fears and panics in the quiet of their own homes? No! So it is "the others" who are the cause of their distress. That seems quite logical. But why stage-fright? Who are "the others" and where does their power lie?

When are you least at your ease in company?

Many people would say:

- When I have to walk in and others are looking at me.
- When I have to speak, even to say something very ordinary.

- When I have to eat with other people.
- As soon as I attract attention. It's ridiculous, but I should be perfectly all right if I could speak from behind a curtain.
- When I'm in the company of the opposite sex.
- When people tease me.
- When it's time for me to go, and I have to get up and leave; it's such torture that I'd rather be called a bore that outstays his welcome.
- When I have to disagree, with what someone has said.
- When I have to express a personal opinion and other people are listening to me in silence.

And so on, and so on.

What do you feel?

- That I look shabby and insignificant.
- Utterly crushed when anyone disagrees with me.
- A longing that some calamity will occur before I have to speak.
- That my memory is useless and that I shan't be able to say a word if once I lose the thread of my argument.
- A panic desire to run away.

- That I'm being misjudged because I'm giving the impression that I'm arrogant, reserved, sullen, incompetent and stupid.
- That every smile has a sneer in it directed at me.

The vicious circle

You're not at your ease with others? So it's *"the other"* who frighten you. Is it normal that you should be afraid of other people? Is it normal that a look, a smile, a gesture from "the others" should so often be interpreted in the worst possible way? My answer is: *It's normal up to a point.* All human beings know what it is to feel they have weaknesses and are inferior to those around them. A human being is essentially weak, and it's only fools who don't know it. But do realize that these pompous people are themselves very weak and by their behaviour are trying to make up for their feelings of inferiority. *A sense of inferiority is like fear. It is inherent in human nature.* And to a certain extent it helps a man to advance in life. How many men would never get anywhere if it weren't for the constant spur provided by the anxiety they feel when they face the many problems that life poses! So a certain amount of fear and anxiety is natural. But why should a man experience a sort of paralysis when a pretty woman looks at him? Why should another go pale when he has to say a few words in public? Why should yet another perspire whenever he must express his opinion before other people?

All these manifestations can be grouped together under one key word-*shyness.*

SHYNESS

Shy people will not contradict me when I say that the misunderstandings caused by this difficulty can be a serious embarrassment! And the trouble can go deeper than that. The shy person knows that "the others" are aware of his affliction. This obviously makes matters worse, causes panic and can have other unfortunate consequences. It will be understood that a slight timidity does not exhibit the same symptoms as an acute attack of stage-fright.

THE SYMPTOMS OF SHYNESS

May I suggest that you put yourself to the test? Read the following questions, which comprise most of the troubles caused by shyness.

Do you experience some of the following symptoms in public or when you are with certain people?

- ▯ Tightening of the chest or muscular contraction?
- ▯ Wobbly legs?

- Drying up of saliva?
- Excessive sweating?
- A feeling that your heart is going to give out?
- Stiffening of the body, hesitant movements?
- Trembling in the legs, hands, lips?
- A feeling that your face is getting red or going pale?
- A "block" in your thoughts and ideas?
- Talking unnaturally faster, your words getting out of control?

In the same circumstances, do you experience some of the following:

- The feeling that you're inferior to everyone else, that everything's on top of you?
- Sudden aggressiveness so that you make exaggerated gestures to back up what you're saying?
- The vague feeling that you're guilty of something?
- The impression that people are ill-disposed to you, that they find fault with you?
- The feeling that others are condescending towards you?

- The impression that your superior thinks little of you?
- The impression that those under you make fun of you?
- The conviction that an encouraging word would change everything?
- The inability to reply to a compliment as well as you can to an attack?
- A fear of contradicting others or of expressing your own opinion?
- A vague feeling that you're too pleasant, too polite, too courteous?
- The feeling that some mysterious force is always holding you back, and that an uneasiness you can't pin down is always with you?
- The impression that you are in danger?
- A constant fear of ridicule, a feeling that you're always awkward?
- A feeling that when other people smile they are being condescendingly amused at your clumsiness?
- A feeling that it's impossible for you to be yourself for fear of making a bad impression?
- The feeling that everything's going to pieces

and that you're completely losing control of yourself?

If you have answered "yes" to even some of these questions, you can take your place in the vast army of the shy.

If so, what should you do? Go on reading this book!

THE EFFECTS AND COUNTER-EFFECTS OF SHYNESS

Shyness can make shambles of lives. It prevents many lives from developing. It represses or stunts superior minds. It cancels out the efforts of people who would be capable of climbing to the highest positions. It prevents intelligent people from getting ahead, from becoming real leaders, from putting their ideas forward and making themselves felt.

▯ *Being shy?* said one man to me. *It means being afraid all the time. It means having to say "all right" to everything other people say. Often it means making tremendous efforts to overcome your shyness, with the sole result that you're taken for a milksop or a coward. When I'm with other people all my wits and intelligence desert me. I never dare say what I know and give myself a chance! This also means that I seem to others to lack the courage of my convictions but to express an opinion one has to be bold. And I don't dare. The sight of one of my superiors paralyses me. The only thing that doesn't give me this absurd feeling of timidity is to keep my mouth shut and nod my head. And then afterwards for days on end I kick myself morally and tell myself that next time they'll see! And the next time, it starts all over again. I'm forty, and shyness has always clung to me like my shadow. To be with other people is a nightmare for me. My timidity has become a real obsession, almost a way of life. To think what I could have done if I hadn't been shy!*

So shyness makes many people unhappy. Yet they dream all the time of making friends. On the other hand they isolate themselves and fail to find the sympathy they need more than anything else.

Why? Because they don't speak or express their feelings. It's all too well known that as a result they suffer cruelly, and perpetually!

Before we go any further, what are the principal effects of shyness?

THE PHYSICAL EFFECTS

Fear

Fear is the most dominant factor in shyness, sometimes this stays under the surface, producing a perpetual feeling of uneasiness and anxiety. Sometimes it makes itself more clearly felt, and causes constriction in the throat, or around the heart and a hollow feeling in the stomach. I shall come back to this later.

Difficulty in speaking

Timid people usually suffer from difficult or painful breathing. This is caused by constriction in the chest, as a result of which the spoken word comes out weak, shaky, in fits and starts. The vocal chords become taut. The tone of the voice changes and often becomes shrill and penetrating (although plenty of shy people have heavy, monotonous). Some of them stammer or talk unintelligibly, because their face muscles stiffen and prevent them from articulating properly.

Muscular contractions

We all know that shy people are awkward when they are in company. They "fluff" their entries, knock into furniture, upset their glasses onto the tablecloth, spill food from their plates, and so on. They suffer from stiffening of the muscles which hinders their movements. Moreover, the shy person knows—or believes—he is being looked at: his legs stiffen, he drags his feet, his fingers tremble.

Tiredness

Apart from permanent fatigue, which highly-strung people suffer from (and among these there are a lot of shy people—see page 23), a shy person experiences great exhaustion after an attack of stage-fright. Often he gets scared about this when there in no need to: the feeling of tiredness comes quite simply from a general state of muscular contraction.

The dulling of the senses

What do some of the shy ones say?

- I have the impression that I no longer feel the objects I touch...
- I think that if someone hit me, I wouldn't feel it...
- Except for the things that frighten me, I see and hear nothing...

This last remark gives us the key to the problem! It is quite true that the timid are oblivious of everything apart from what scares them. This is one of the main characteristics of an attack of stage-fright, for instance. What happens in such cases? Let's imagine a shy person who has to speak in public. A woman, for example, looks at him. The attack of stage-fright starts. At that moment, his fear is centered solely on the woman. He can see only her. All his attention is concentrated on this cause of his fear. Nothing else exists for him, as he sees and hears nothing else. The range of his awareness shrinks-and his sensory perception is reduced accordingly. That is why a timid speaker frequently forgets that he has already dealt with some point or other in his speech.

Vascular troubles

They cause the blushing (or loss of color) from which shy people suffer. It results from dilatation or constriction of the blood-vessels.

Secretory troubles

The saliva ceases to flow and the lips become extremely dry. There is excessive sweating of the hands, and under the armpits.

THE PSYCHOLOGICAL EFFECTS

The feeling of panic

In general, a shy person is a worthy man, and he feels a desperate need that others should appreciate his worth. But, what happens?

- The panic he feels makes him run away as fast as he can. Why? To escape from his panic, that's all!
- On the other hand, he is afraid of social failure. He is constantly afraid of being thought little of by "the others."

This fear pins him down like a butterfly in a glass case.

- As he is hamstrung and unable to move, he obviously cannot control the situation. All the more so, because, as I have already said, he is not aware of anything other than what frightens him. And so he feels weak and defenceless in the face of attack—and for him there are attacks threatening from all quarters! Even while he is forcing himself not to run away, he feels a terrible anxiety growing within him which increases and takes complete possession of him.

Observe that there are shy people who suddenly give up everything. They surrender to panic, and, without any warning, run away—in the middle of a meal or a conversation when you question them point-blank, for instance. This often happens with timid children.

The intellectual enigma

If you question a shy though intelligent person, he will often remain mute. It is as if he were struck dumb. Unless, of course, he breaks into loud laughter—but without venturing a word. He may equally well launch into a flood of jumbled words, very little of which he remembers, once the crisis is past.)

The shy person, then, is dazed. His brain goes numb. His will-power breaks down. He wants to act, but he can't. He may want to make some move, to do or say something—but firm brakes hold him back. *He feels unable to adapt himself—and so he takes refuge in complete passivity, and morally speaking, hides himself so that he won't have to fight.*

You know those shy people who visit you and stay on until an impossibly late hour. "Why does he do it?" you say to yourself, "since he is shy and would like nothing better than to get away?" Exactly! Before he reached your house, that man was trembling. He asked himself—"Shall I go, or not? Then he seized the bull by the horns. He tried to overcome his fear. Now that he's in your house, he's scared of having to speak or draw attention to himself. He burrows down into one of your armchairs. Then it's time to go. So he's going to have to get up, say a few polite words of thanks. He's going to have to bow, smile, speak graciously. Now, he is afraid of attracting attention and this is precisely what he's going to have to do if he wants to go! He keeps quiet and submits to the torment. He is held down, silent and stiff. He mutters vague monosyllables and waits, hoping that something unexpected will happen to deliver him from his martyrdom. And you—you probably, curse him instead of understanding him and helping him.

In short...

The way a shy person behaves in company can be summed up thus. An inability to adapt himself. He should be able to take things in his stride. He should be able to walk, move about, greet people, talk and express ideas. But he is completely incapable of doing these things because of his fear and his emotional state. In the presence of others, he becomes a kind of machine and turns into an automaton. He is governed by reflexes and habits, when he should be using his judgment and his will—which of course, are inhibited by his timidity!

The shy person is afraid in company. Why? What danger is he facing? Simply that of being unappreciated or misjudged. He feels weak and knows that his weakness and inner paralysis are leading him towards failure.

CLASSIFICATION

The human temperament can be classified under six main headings. But most shy people are found in the following three:

- **The sensitive.** Very easily upset, he is fastidious preposterously idealistic, introverted, with a difficult and very emotional character. Moreover—and above all—the sensitive person is **non-active.**

- **The highly-strung.** Very unstable, he is impulsive, changeable, emotional. He too is **non-active.**

- **The impetuous.** He is hot-blooded, ambitious, violent, uncompromising both with himself and others, idealistic, emotional—but the impetuous type is **active.**

It is among these three human types that most shy people are found. I mean people who are shy by nature, whose shyness is a part of their personality, rather than those who have been robbed of their confidence by circumstances.

I will list five other types of temperament, but only by way of information as inborn shyness is hardly ever part of their make-up:

- The bad-tempered
- The phlegmatic
- The sanguine
- The apathetic
- The nondescript.

ON THE TRAIL

When we look into the matter of shyness, we find that it is often met with among the first three human types but especially:

- Among sensitive people.
- Among the highly-strung.

Why less among the impetuous? *Because they are capable of action.*

- **The sensitive person is,** essentially, defenceless

against life. His sensitiveness is too acute. The merest thing wounds him deeply. He broods and is often misanthropic. He is harrowed by a feeling of inferiority. His shyness sticks to him like glue, and is almost as much a part of him as his blood. And, especially, *he is incapable of action!*

▯ **The highly-strung person** can be recognized by the following symptoms: tiredness, irritability, exaggerated emotion, instability, introspection, impressionability, dreaminess and a vivid imagination. Like the sensitive person, *he finds it difficult to take action,* except in sudden flurries. We cannot say that his shyness goes as deep as that of the sensitive person, but those who are highly-strung have a strong tendency to general shyness.

Let us draw a first conclusion

- Most shy people are to be found among the sentimental and the highly-strung.
- Shyness is an inborn characteristic of sentimental people and of many highly-strung people.
- Nevertheless, many of the timid ones are neither sentimental nor highly-strung. These owe their shyness not to their temperament, but to certain circumstances and the way they have reacted to them.

Let's take, for example, a *phlegmatic person.* By temperament he is magnificently even-tempered. He is tolerant, unflustered and active. He is not excessively emotional. Is he likely to be innately shy? Not at all! But if he is shy nevertheless? Well, one can be quite certain that *he has become so.* As the result of circumstances, perhaps because of upbringing, emotional shocks, or maybe repeated failures. Please remember, by the way, that I am speaking here of those who are phlegmatic by nature, and not of those who deliberately control themselves, foolishly considering it their duty to keep calm under all circumstances.

The sensitive, the highly-strung and the shy

Here is a table which shows:

- A comparison between the sensitive and highly-strung, and those who are shy.
- The normal reactions of the shy, whatever their temperament may be.

SENSITIVE AND HIGHLY-STRUNG

- Very emotional
- Their emotional state is complicated by an inability to act.
- They turn away from society and are given to constant analysing of themselves. They brood.

- They become misanthropic and fiercely individualistic.
- They are often ambitious, intelligent and proud.
- Believing they are made differently from other people, they become surly, morose and generally difficult.
- They suffer a great deal from their inability to act.
- They are often extremely honest and highly moral.

SHY

- Nearly always very emotional—whether by temperament or because they have become so.
- Often pessimistic, they are convinced everything will go badly for them and so they avoid action.

  They withdraw within themselves.
- They brood over their repeated failures, thus making their shyness worse.
- Since they are afraid, they are obliged to live apart from society.
- They know they have ability, but being incapable of putting it to use they become arrogant.

- They often counterbalance their fear by taking refuge in bad temper, insolence and impulsiveness that is sometimes violent.
- They are always angry with themselves because of their fear of taking action.
- They are afraid they will not be able to perform their tasks properly.

What does all this show? That the sentimental, the highly-strung and the shy run a great risk—that of becoming *resigned;* Why? Because they are convinced they will be social failures! This is why a shy person will often refuse to appear in public by saying:

"What is the use? I'm quite certain people will think me incompetent and awkward-so I'd rather stay at home and not make an exhibition of myself!"

So many shy people are resigned to their state. But they resign themselves *in advance!* And that's where they go wrong. They fail before they start because of their fear of failure!

And they also say:

"When things have gone wrong several times, one gives up trying. Every time I open my mouth in company, it's a disaster so why should I force myself to do it again?"

Just a moment! We should not imagine that shyness is *only* to be found among the sentimental and the highly-strung (as I have already pointed out). It can attack all types of people as a result of various circumstances.

For example, glance at the definition of *"the impetuous type"* on page 20 and suppose that as a result of certain circumstances, he becomes incapable of taking the bull by the horns—that is to say, of acting. He will find himself still with his ambition, his violence, his idealism and his emotions. *But he will no longer have the benefit of action as a safety-valve.* He will quickly become like the sentimental and highly-strung, and will then have every chance of becoming shy!

Some other important characteristics of shyness

Because of his emotional state, the shy person is, as we know, very much at the mercy of events.

Now, we also know that he is inactive. And so instead of being channelled into action, his emotions flow around and around inside him. You might say they battle against the current, instead of going with it.

Therefore a shy person who plunges into action often finds that his trouble is over.

Shyness has other characteristics:

- Indecision, constant hesitation, depression,

- Gloominess, anger against oneself, hatred of shyness.
- Lack of confidence in oneself—which leads to a craving for protection from others.
- A desire for complete solitude, to shelter oneself from the world.

The shy person's double game

The shy fear society and yet they always come back to it. Why? Simply because:

- They feel a tremendous need to be loved.
- They feel a tremendous need to love.

So they seek the company of others, while at the same time they are continually troubled and hurt by them!

Since the shy person is often inactive, he becomes awkward and terribly clumsy. His emotional state and his anxiety prevent him from *doing things spontaneously and easily.* Perhaps we often think it is easy to express sincere and deeply felt sentiments. But look at most people —as soon as they have to express such things, they become awkward. They splutter, become moist-eyed, smile pathetically, gesticulate, blush, go pale, become curt of gruff, and show every sign of wanting to run away. And this is normal. Nothing is more difficult than to express deep feelings *naturally,* because emotion always comes into it. *To seem natural and spontaneous requires great qualities* which only go with a balanced personality. To express deeply-felt-sentiments—love, goodness, brotherhood, justice, fellow-feeling, affection for example—demands inward calm or otherwise emotion will choke the expression of these feelings! One has to learn how to choose one's words and gestures carefully and to be master of one's tongue. So, I repeat, don't let emotion overcome you.

Otherwise, what happens? (And this is one is one of the characteristics of the shy person when he is in company):

- Emotion twists the feelings. If an emotional person tries to express deeply-felt sentiments, his personality appears to change! His emotion not only paralyses him, but throws his personality completely out of gear. His emotions are like a *tidal wave inside him.* I shall return to this subject (page 56).

- As a result of his emotional state, he becomes on the defensive. He worries about his dignity. He becomes cold, reserved, distant and haughty. And so it becomes a question of probing into the deep feelings of the emotional person—which is very difficult for anyone other than an expert. These defence barriers put up against an emotional state always make a bad impression in company, where human relations are on the surface.

So this is what happens:

- The shy (or emotional) person's attempts to be spontaneous only result in a lack of spontaneity.
- This lack of spontaneity becomes an attitude of curt chilliness.
- Faced by his haughty coldness, others turn away.
- He is wounded when this happens.
- He suffers when others fail to understand his true feelings, although he does everything possible to hide them.
- When, in the end, he finds himself alone, he is terribly distressed.

The shy person is vulnerable

He is like a castle with a thousand openings through which one can easily short hundreds of arrows.

And so:

- Since he is vulnerable, he is defenceless when attacked.
- He is incapable of reacting quickly.

- Being inactive, he is robbed of means of defence.

- He always feels threatened, even if no one wants to hurt him.

This last point is important! It is certainly true that modern life is bewildering. So many people treat one another like objects or machines. They are concerned above all with profits, productivity, dynamism and work. So men withdraw into their unconcern and indifference to others. The shy person is too sensitive to accept such a way of life. This lack of feeling is intolerable to him. *since it revolts him, he should do something about it!* He should be able to say what he thinks, hammer his fist on the table and protest against the lack of human feeling which so appals; him *but he does nothing-because his shyness has condemned him to inactivity.*

So what does he do? What he always does: he hates his inability to take action and he retires into loneliness. Not for long however! He comes back into society because he needs to love and be loved, as I have already said.

And then?

- He gets the impression that he is unwanted. He feels he is being tolerated, allowed in – but no more.

- He thinks he is the focus of attention and that he is being judged unfavorably.
- So he does everything he can to find out what other people think of him. He watches for the slightest indication and notes it down carefully at the back of his mind so that he can chew it over later. Not a gesture, not a word, not a smile, not a look escapes him!

Yet more contradictions

- On the one hand, the shy person suffers from being (or so he thinks) the centre of interest.
- On the other hand he hates indifference and therefore he cannot conceive why they should not be interested in him. As he believes that the only reason why people take an interest in him is so that they can pass judgment on him, he puts the worst possible interpretation on everything!

In addition:

- The shy person is very clumsy in dealing with others.
- But he expects the greatest tact and delicacy when they have anything to do with him.

So:

- It is very difficult not to wound a shy person (useless to ask yourself how you managed to annoy him!).
- Feeling hurt, he becomes hostile towards others. The others wonder why he turns away; they are sometimes astonished to learn that they said such and such a thing, which they had not meant, in any case, in any unkind way.

The shy person broods

In company he is always on the watch, as I have said. The circumstances that have produced his fear are impressed on his mind. He sees nothing else and notes every trifling detail. He will be struck by a mere inflection in someone's voice, a smile, a look. What does he do then? At that moment, these details seem insignificant to him, *as, in fact, they are!* But little by little he starts turning them over in his mind. They snowball, become important and, in the end, take on meanings that are as various as they are unreal. Day after day, the wound gets deeper.

The mechanism functions in two stages:

- When he leaves the others, he will say to himself: "I thought Mr. X was a bit distant today. "But at the time he is not hurt at this, hardly surprised. He arrives home and it is then that the second stage gets under way.

- He broods and looks for hidden meanings. "Mr. X's coldness," he says to himself "was probably a cover-up for his dislike of me. I wonder why? He goes on turning it over. He strains to remember. Detail piles up on detail. He starts building with them. "I must have been clumsy. Or was I stupid? Unless X is horribly sly. Ah, he hides his hand well! If only I'd retorted with this or that! But I swear that next time I see him I'll tell him what I think!"

You can be certain that he'll do nothing about it, and that the merest friendly smile from Mr. X will sweep away his broodings in a second.

So:

- The shy person thinks he is protecting himself by with-drawing into his shell.
- In this shell, his imagination will only feed on itself, which will hurt him rather than protect him.

Chapter II

The Manifestations of Shyness

STAGE-FRIGHT

Stage-fright can be regarded as an acute attack of shyness. It has the same symptoms-at their most severe-as ordinary shyness. How many celebrated speakers and actors are subject to it! And the fact that these men are famous, admired and certain of their success, doesn't stop the onset of stage-fright. *One can therefore see, that the trouble comes from deep down; and that stage-fright is only a symptom of something else—* just as an ulcer is only a symptom of hyperacidity of the stomach.

The physical effects of an attack of stage-fright are very marked; cold sweat, diarrhoea, vomiting, palpitations, flutterings of the heart. And, often, total loss of memory.

An attack of stage-fright often resolves itself as follows;

- Either the attack fades when the action has got under way

or

- The sufferer is compelled to break off suddenly from what he has begun.

What sometimes happens: The actor, having lost his memory completely, the prompter cannot help him and he is obliged to leave the stage. Or a lecturer's panic obliges him to skip an important part of his text.

What do those who suffer from stage-fright say?

"The sight of the audience is enough to make me tremble. Why? I've no idea—but one thing that terrifies me is the fact that everyone is so still. If I could speak while walking up and down and making gestures, and if the audience would move a bit instead of staring at me, I don't think stage-fright would trouble me. But, as it is, I have the impression that I'm before a tribunal specially assembled to judge whether I'm any good. Then my faith in my ability sinks almost to zero!".

"The fact of *seeing* the audience lets loose a violent upsurge of emotion in me. It's ridiculous, but if I could speak while hidden behind a curtain, I should be completely at ease. In company I've a dread of being a disappointment, of being taken for a nobody, boring people and irritating them. This feeling of being thrown to the lions never leaves me.

And so I am brusque and curt in an attempt to break the spell I'm under..."

"As you know, I'm a well-known lawyer and yet it's as if I were putting my whole reputation at stake every time. This applies whether I'm pleading a case or talking at a cocktail party. The presence of others saps my self-confidence..."

"When I go for an oral examination, the professor's composure makes me go to pieces. I've covered the course very thoroughly, and yet I automatically lose my memory. I rack my brains—but there's nothing. An empty well. And panicky fear. My hands run with sweat, my legs wobble! My last 'oral' was a disaster I had to walk out in the middle of the questions. The professor dismissed me, and two other students had to support me. I was a wreck for two days..."

Accompanying these physical manifestation of stage-fright, there are generally two psychological ones:

- The shy person remembers nothing—or very little—of what happened during the attack of stage-fright.
- During the attack he acts subconsciously and automatically.

SEXUAL SHYNESS

This type of shyness is both common and normal in adolescents. Adolescence stimulates the emotional capacity. This emotion is concentrated on a factor that is completely new for the adolescent: sexuality. Adolescent timidity is more prevalent in boys than in girls. Why? Because the boys have to take the first step towards the opposite sex. As for the girls, they are happy enough to wait for the attentions they think they are entitled to—and which they intend to have. So adolescent males find themselves in a dilemma:

- They are tongue-tied in female company.
- At the same time, they feel they must serve their apprenticeship in social behavior towards women.

That is why awkwardness and bad manners are often the lot of adolescents. They remain seated in a bus while a woman is standing up. Boorishness? Not at all-timidity, shyness.

And you see a little farce being enacted between boys and girls:

- The boys feel clumsy and awkward, and show it by a sort of anti-feminine attitude.
- The girls hide their own shyness by an attitude of mockery and disdain.

So what happens if the adolescent state lasts too long? If a man doesn't manage to jump the ditch that separates him from adulthood? Just this: the basically sexual shyness continues. This causes (it goes without saying) sexual difficulties. This prolonged adolescence will have its influence on everything he does in life.

If a man remains mentally tied to his adolescence, he will emerge physically into adulthood but psychologically will be left behind! *The whole of his social life will be affected.* Naturally, he will be afraid of women. He may even come to hate them—because he fears them, of course. Feelings of inferiority will develop and will stretch their tentacles everywhere. His shyness will become all—embracing. He will be constantly haunted by a feeling of guilt, of making a bad impression. He will be convinced that whatever he does in the future will be a failure, whether it concerns sex or his place in society. One can see that this sort of shyness can be caused by numerous factors, and I will come back to them later.

FALSE SHYNESS

What does a shy person do but hate his shyness so he tries to find out what causes it! Sometimes he succeeds (or thinks he does).

This is what some of these people say:

- I'm shy because I stammer (when really he stammers because he is shy).
- It's my prominent ears that make me shy.
- I became shy because of my small stature.
- We were poor, but I went to a school where there were lots of children of rich parents.
- My forehead is pimply and I've got a bad skin.
- I've got big feet and their clumsiness is so obvious.
- My hands are large and my nails are unsightly.
- I'm ashamed of what I do in private and feel that everyone present knows about it.
- I'm fat and tubby.
- I get afraid when I have to give orders to my subordinates, and I have to hide my shyness by being curt. But I'm always scared I won't manage to act as they expect me to and I shall lose the prestige that a manager should enjoy. At such times I always feel that I would rather take orders than give them.

What does all this mean? As I said, the shy person is always trying to find out what makes him shy. And this is natural. But unfortunately he sidetracks the issue nine times out of ten.

The reasons that these men give for their timidity

are not the real ones. I'll come back to the subject, but I can say this much now: if these people had been *properly balanced at the outset,* they would never have become victims of shyness, in spite of this one's smallness and that one's bad skin.

But when another one says, "I get the impression that everyone knows about what I do in private, "he is putting his finger on the root cause of his shyness-which, by the way, has nothing to do with timidity but is an *obsession of guilt.* I'll come back to this, too; and we shall see that the problem of shyness isn't as simple as many people think.

TEMPORARY SHYNESS

If you're shy, it's because you can't adapt yourself to the circumstances in which you find yourself. You are caught off guard. In order to be immune to shyness, you have to be able to *adapt yourself immediately and completely* to any and all circumstances.

For instance: If someone has never been to a big dinner-party before, and doesn't know how to use certain forks or spoons or how to tackle certain dishes, it will be practically impossible for him to adapt himself immediately to all the things that are new to him. So there is every chance he will feel shy. If, during the course of the meal, he keeps his eyes open and observes what others do and keeps more or less calm, he will gradually adapt himself and his temporary shyness will disappear.

Shedding temporary shyness therefore depends on accustoming oneself to circumstances. It is pretty certain that after attending two or three more such parties that person will have thrown off his shyness.

In conclusion

As I have already said, shyness is nearly always a symptom of a deeper psychological trouble.

If someone goes to a psychologist and says, *"I want you to cure me of my shyness..."*

...the psychologist will at once say to himself:

"I must try to find out what it is that deep down is causing the shyness. And it's quite likely that the real trouble has got nothing to do with shyness in the true sense of the word..."

IS SHYNESS AN ILLNESS?

Without any hesitation, I say "yes." At any rate, in the majority of cases. It is certainly a symptom of psychological illness.

Those who are really shy will agree with me. They know that their illness brings them failure, prevents them from being able to fight when they should, so that they seem stupid and cowardly to those who really have courage. Many shy people can't make friends. Others stay unmarried all their lives. Some live solitary, empty lives. Professional careers can be ruined.

Shy people feel this fear and numbness eating away at them and undermining everything they do. A look from someone and their best resolutions crumble. A smile and their plans (carefully laid in solitude) go adrift.

One can see, then, that real shyness has nothing to do with the mere blushing awkwardness of adolescents. Do not forget that real shyness brings about *permanent* troubles, if only because of the numbing dread it causes from morning to night. *For the really shy person lives in continual fear.* It's a vague fear that can't be pinned down, but an anxious fear all the same. How many employees are there who work admirable well because subconsciously they are afraid of reproof or reprimand—afraid of life, afraid of other people, afraid of superiors, afraid of subordinates, afraid of everything and nothing...

Shyness ruins all plans for social life,. The shy person surrenders, bound hand and foot,. *He can't be a social success* for the very good reason that he is not a success in any other way and his personality is crippled.

His will (even if deep down it is very strong, as is often the case) is shattered when he comes into contact with others. The same is true of his ability to act. A wonderful career could be before him but he will never enjoy it, because he is timid.

Timidity and shame

Fear and shame—the two great ills that torment the shy! Shame shows itself by blushing (sometimes). By confusion (always). Because the shy are often very good observers of themselves they pass judgment on themselves and find themselves ridiculous. The fact that they are ridiculous is something they feel guilty about. This means that they attach far greater importance to other people than those others generally deserve.

Why are they ashamed? There are many possible reasons. Perhaps they feel ashamed because of a subconscious feeling of guilt (but this is a special case, which I'll come back to later.) Generally speaking, the shy person feel ashamed because he feels that in the eyes of others he is thought to be worthless.

THE OBVERSE SIDE OF SHYNESS

Look at that man holding forth on the other side of the room! He holds himself as straight as a ramrod. He stands with his back to the fireplace, speaks loud and clear, with trenchant gestures, dominating his audience with his gaze.

You say to yourself, "How sure of himself that man is!" But perhaps you revise your opinion and say, "That man seems *too* sure of himself! "And you would then be right. Because there is a whole category of people on whom shyness seems to have put on a mask. These are braggarts and blusterers "compensating" for their timidity.

What are they like? They are like animals which, cornered and trembling with fear, suddenly bare their teeth and leap at your throat.

What is meant by "compensation?"

Do you think Bonaparte would have become Napoleon if he had not constantly brooded over his unhappy childhood? Or that Hitler would have become the abominable dictator of the Third Reich if he had not brooded over the emotional frustrations of his early days? Or that Goebbels would have become the evil genius of the same Reich if he had not been afflicted by a club-foot? Or the little workman over there—would he have become a foreman if, in his mind, he were not getting his own back for having been humiliated for years? And what about that other man who climbed to fame and fortune because he knew wretchedness and poverty as a child?

What does all this show? *That when a man has been made to feel inferior, he seeks afterwards to dominate.* That a man who has been humiliated tries to humiliate others in turn. That a poor man tries to become rich and powerful so that he can trample on others and so on.

That's normal, you say? Not so fast! We must see whether redressing the balance in this way serves a useful purpose or is harmful. But first...

Biological compensation

I am touching on this so that we can then see more clearly the same mechanism at work in the psychological domain.

Compensation, says Claparede, *is a means employed by nature to remedy a deficiency in the system and, as well as it can, to restore its normal equilibrium. If a man has one leg too short, which makes him lean to one side, the spinal column will have a "compensation" curve. An injured heart will hypertrophy in order to make up in quantity what it lacks in quality.*

Doctors have always known of this reaction.

What did Goeth say-Goeth who was a great psychologist before the word was used in its modern sense?

If you find that a person has some special quality or

strength, ask yourself immediately in what other respect he is lacking; you will soon find the key to culture!

IN PSYCHOLOGICAL TERMS

The person who feels inferior, for whatever reason, can react in two ways:

1) By running away from whatever it is that frightens him. He gives way to panic, retires into solitude, throws in the towel and is permanently discouraged. This is what one could call a *decompensation.*

2) He can react positively, but in doing so *go too far,* When this happens there is *compensation* (what is also called over-compensation). And this, of course, is a defence mechanism. He dons his armour. He hides his fear under a swaggering exterior.

These two mechanisms have been called fleeing backwards and fleeing forwards. And this is very true. One has seen this in all the wars. Those who run away are called cowards but some who rush forward—goaded by fear—are called heroes, although very often scarcely know what they are doing.

Cyrano de Bergerac

No one would deny that Cyrano de Bergerac is a perfect example of the brilliant, cocksure man of the world. And yet...

Cyrano de Bergerac is neurotic. He is tormented by the fact that he has a very long nose. His nose is, shall we say, his weak point. He has only to see the shadow of his profile on the garden wall to be reminded of his deformity. But just one word "against his nose" and Cyrano draws his sword to pin the insolent fellow to the wall!

On the other hand, our Cyrano is desperately proud of this nose, this cross that he has to bear. You know the long speech in the first act of Rostands' play? It is, as one might say, the masterpiece of a masterpiece! But it's also the expression of a "compensation. "On the one hand, Cyrano will not tolerate from anybody any mention of his nose. On the other hand he talks about it himself with gusto. In doing so he is expressing an intense shyness and a strong feeling of inferiority (see page 62). How many men there are who behave like Cyrano! They bluster and pose and brag to impress people, and quickly become intolerable.

In social life

Is this shy person who seeks to assert himself really at ease in company? Certainly not. Is it then desirable for a shy person to "compensate" for his shyness? Again no. And yet, you will say, he seems forceful. He is scornful, haughty, sarcastic, brusque, cynical, mocking, sneering, difficult to deal with and all the rest! People are afraid of him, which is all he wants. He, the man who is afraid of others, can make others afraid of him. He thinks he is no longer timid. He often imagines he is at peace with the world. If only this beautiful dream were true!

But deep down a little voice whispers to him. "if only it lasts... " And does it? No. Because sooner or later he comes up against someone who sees right through him—someone who realizes that his self-assurance is only a mask and that the iron mask is made of cardboard. Then the swaggerer collapses like a pack of cards. He caves in all the faster because he *knows full* well that his outward behavior is not backed up by what is going on inside him. He knows this; he knows that his self-assurance is really false and that his forcefulness is a sham.

What does this prove? That this sort of attempt to redress the balance, even if it gives an impression of greater security, is always ill-advised. The shy swaggerer is constantly anxious lest he should lose his mask: this fear only reinforces the anxiety produced by his shyness, and he is always on his guard against anything that could rip off the mask. He is like a criminal who has not made a very good job of disguising himself and sees, at the other end of the street, a police patrol.

In everyday life

These shy swaggerers are to be met every day. You know them, just as I do—surly or silent, disliking conversation. They are stiff and curt because they are incapable of expressing goodwill. To show their better feelings is beyond them because it would release the emotional side of their characters.

If this swaggerer feels more at his ease in company, he can be certain that his compensation will one day rebound on him, because he is not pleasant to look at or to listen to. He seems to be hostile to everyone and everything, which makes him a profoundly unattractive person in the eyes of those who cannot see further than the end of their noses. So this sort of shyness is as unpleasant for the man himself as it is for those around him.

THE EMOTIONAL STATE

Are you...

- ▯ Easily tired?
- ▯ Tired in the morning but lively in the evening?
- ▯ Irritable?
- ▯ Moody?
- ▯ Hypersensitive to pain?
- ▯ Put out by the slightest thing?

- Subject to vague nagging pains similar to neuralgia?
- Subject to pains in the nape of the neck after an outburst of emotion?
- Very suspicious?
- Inclined to enjoy being miserable?
- Very jealous?
- Very impressionable and easily led?
- Apt to worry about yourself whenever people talk about illnesses?
- Subject to sudden lapses of memory?
- Inclined to work in fits and starts?
- Irritable? Do you look for a quarrel over nothing, especially in the morning?
- Subject to spasms, trembling, twitching eyelids?
- Sometimes seized by the feeling that you've lost your bearings?
- Subject to intellectual lapses for which there is no apparent reason?

These are all characteristics of emotional people, who are part of the immense family of the highly-strung. They are consequently in the same family as those who are *never* at their ease in company because they can never relax.

Who is emotional?

The answer is simple—*everyone is!* We all have emotion in our make-up. How much we have varies considerably according to our temperaments and circumstances. What we should know is when that quality of emotion goes beyond the normal. Many people complain of being emotional! They suffer because of it and dread their weakness like the plague. Why? Because they feel incapable of restraining and controlling themselves.

That is why it is essential to notice the difference between *emotion* (normal) and hyper-emotion or excessive emotion (abnormal).

WHAT IS EMOTION?

It is a fundamental characteristic of all human beings—and of animals too. It is because of this quality that we *react* to physical stimulants or to changes in our bodily or mental situation. Emotion is the *most elementary aspect* of the human being. It actuates the body to seek out what is agreable, and to flee from (or to counter-attack) what is disagreeable. It is then that we experience the sensations of pleasure, elation, well-being, fear, panic, and such.

You find yourself for instance, in the company of several people. Without being prepared for it, you are called upon to walk round, to chat and to introduce people to one another. What do all these actions mean to you if you are shy? They mean *danger,* a situation that suddenly comes on you with no warning-and while other people are watching you. *It is this feeling of danger which constitutes emotion in the true sense of the word.* In such a case, what are you going to do? As there is danger, you are going to try and eliminate it, because the sensation it gives you is disagreeable.

How will you eliminate it? There are two basic solutions.

- Either you will run away—in this way you eliminate the danger by disappearing from the scene.

or

- You will become aggressive—thus eliminating the danger by counter-attacking.

But if you are a balanced person.

- You will notice one by one the elements that constitute this danger.
- You will gradually adapt yourself to them.
- In the end you will get used to the situation and will do what is expected of you.

And in doing all this, you will feel emotion? Yes, of course! But your emotion will be *channelled* and *restrained* by your balanced judgment.

How can one learn to control one's emotions without inordinate effort? That is indeed an important question. It is the key to success in being at ease in the company of others.

An ideal within the reach of everyone

The ideal, then, is to be able to control our emotions without appearing either timid or aggressive. But how? By gritting the teeth and clenching the fists? By subduing or humbling ourselves? I know that these methods are often extolled in the name of "self-discipline" and" human dignity." But I maintain that they do a lot of harm and very little good. In any case, forcing ourselves into a strait-jacket is, and will always be, *a false kind of self-discipline* just as an obsessive concentration on some target or other can be a false exercise of will-power. Will-power and self-discipline are only genuine when they are the natural outcome of an organism that is functioning smoothly, and are not produced by obstinacy and self-will.

Where does it come from this emotion that is sometimes violent and prevents so many people from achieving their aims? What are its effects? How are we to prevent it from doing harm?

THE BRAIN

Rest assured, emotion doesn't come from the moon. Its source is in the very important nerve centres situated at the base of the brain. That great organ of the body we call the brain has two principal areas.

- *The lower area.* This is the area of the emotions, instincts, habits, forgotten memories and moods. In other words, it is the centre of our most basic and uncontrollable reactions. It is, in fact, the area of the subconscious-an area that is a fantastic complex of glands and nerves. On it depends the smooth (or otherwise) functioning of our sympathetic nervous system-on which depends, in its turn, the more or less harmonious functioning of our internal organs;
- *The upper area.* This is the outer grey matter of the brain called the cerebral cortex. I do not say that this is centre of consciousness and will. But these do depend on the smooth functioning of the cortex and it is essential that this mechanism should be in good order, so that the wheels will turn without creaking or stopping altogether!

What happens then?

- The lower and upper areas are in continual communication (through nerve channels) and constantly exchange messages.
- These communications must flow smoothly, otherwise one area will take the lead of the other and assume the ascendancy.

- If the cerebral cortex is weakened, the lower area will get the upper hand. It can often be noticed that a weakness of the cortex (resulting from fatigue for example) unleashes the lower area. Result-emotion, anger, passion and the like.
- We also know that if the cerebral cortex is functioning smoothly, it serves as a *brake* on the undisciplined tendencies of the lower area.

In company, for instance...

- You have to speak, but you are very tired (or worried or whatever it may be). Normally you are not emotional.
- This tiredness affects the cortex and reduces its natural power.
- As it is tired, the cortex hasn't the necessary strength to resist the lower area.
- This lower area lets loose violent emotion.
- The expression of this emotion appears without your being able to do anything about it, *because your brakes are slack...*

Suppose....

Suppose now that you possessed some magic device which would make your cortex function smoothly again. What would happen?

The brakes would grip again. The confusion stemming from the subconscious would disappear, together with your emotion. Your control would immediately be re-established.

Do realize how important it is that the cortex should function smoothly. Your brain must receive the same care and attention as the other organs of your body.

ARE YOU TOO EMOTIONAL?

Emotion is normal. But when? *When its intensity and duration are in proportion to the circumstances that have produced it.*

You are in the street, for instance. You suddenly see an accident. A confused din, smashed cars. But no one is killed or injured. Normally the emotion produced by a shock like this should disappear very quickly. But an over-sensitive person will still be trembling inwardly half an hour later, and will show all the physical signs of emotion—pallor, trembling, shaky legs, and floods of words. He has not "digested" the emotional shock.

Excessive emotion is a tidal wave

Too often we fail to realize that violent emotion reacts on *the whole* of the organism—heart, kidneys, brain—producing a variety of vasomotor and glandular effects. These include redness or paleness of the hands and face, cold shivers, numbness in the extremities (sometimes the hands feel dead); a heaviness like a dead weight on the eyelids, a painful stiffness in the nape of the neck, sudden speeding up of the pulse, waves of heat through the body. All of these symptoms can be observed in people who are victims of violent emotion.

Such symptoms are received by the victim with acute alarm, panic.

But we must realize that...

- All these manifestations are only reflexes that occur in everyone. They are basic nervous reactions by means of which the organism keeps itself on an even keel.

They are caused by highly sensitive vasomotor nerves. Unfortunately, highly-strung people look on them as terrible misfortunes.

A surplus of emotion

- A hyperemotional person goes to a theatre, a cinema, a reception, a party. What happens? His emotional feelings well up inside him, disturbing his whole system, including his brain, *so the cerebral cortex ceases to function smoothly.*

- The way is then open for the troubles that come from the brain's lower area. State-fright and panic set in.
- Other troubles arise also—palpitations, for example. These palpitations give rise to fear, and the over-emotional person is then gripped by the feeling that he is about to faint, to choke, to suffocate. He begins to feel ill. He needs air, his heart thumps and he is seized by a dreadful fear.
- This fear makes him want to run away. Why? To rid himself of the fear!
- If he escapes and gets away, he experiences immediate relief.

But...!

He was seized by "fear" and the fear will remain imprinted on the subconscious areas of his brain. If he returns later to the same place, the chain-reaction will again occur—and this time it will be worse because of his memories of the first experience. This time he may sit near the door, so that if the dreaded moment comes it will be easy for him to get away before real panic sets in.

Thus it is that very many over-emotional people have a real terror of certain public places—such as churches and theatres. They invent a thousand excuses to avoid them, but hide the real reason because they are ashamed of it, although they would feel far less shame if only other people could understand them a little.

The stage that over-emotional people get into in the company of others can be compared with a photographic plate on to which all impressions are projected and fixed. Two important characteristics of over-emotional people are *perpetual hesitancy and doubt.* These sometimes reach such an intensity that the simplest problems turn into a torment of uncertainty and debate.

Doubt is a characteristic of the over-emotional. In company or with their families, they become hesitant, indecisive, irresolute, timid, suspicious, easily annoyed. A trifling thing will make them jealous. They are irritable with those who are nearest and dearest to them, sometimes to the point of hatred. They brood all night over little things of no importance—about remarks people have made to them which they interpret as a personal insult and an affront to their dignity.

Their over-sensitivity keeps them watchful and suspicious all the time. They are at the mercy of every current, swept this way and that. The smallest thing can fill them with joy but a trifle can plunge them into despair or bitterness. If a man of this kind is in direct and constant contact with his boss, this can constitute a worry which can result in insomnia, irritability and general fatigue. Its inevitable that they cannot adapt themselves to the society around them and in which they have to live.

FEAR

The is another great cause of the inability of individuals to adapt themselves to society.

I have said that all human beings experience emotion, to a greater or lesser extent. This is equally true of fear. Fear is part of the human make-up, for humans find themselves up against thousands of problems that are beyond their understanding. *So we must draw a line between normal fear and pathological fear.*

In fact, fear is on two levels—anxiety, and fear in the true sense of the word.

Anxiety

Anxiety is psychological.

- The person subject to anxiety has the feeling of *imminent danger.* It is a danger he is unable to define but it weighs heavily on him. This feeling is accentuated by a vivid imagination. As a consequence for instance, of his feeling that some indefinable danger is imminent, he will imagine that when he gets back home he will find his house in flames, and his wife and children suffocated.

- This person is in a constant state of alert and is obsessed by it. He can think of nothing else but the catastrophe that threatens him and in consequence he is continually losing the thread of his ideas, his thoughts and his conversation.
- He feels helpless before this danger-just like the shy person, you will notice. And this feeling of complete impotence throws him completely out of gear.

Fear in the true sense

When anxiety really takes hold, certain physical phenomena appear and these are the signs of fear.

There is:

- Difficult or labored breathing (dysponea).
- Acceleration or slowing down of the pulse.
- Violent contractions of the facial or neck muscles, wild looking eyes, half-open mouth, dryness in the mouth and sweating.

You will notice that these symptoms correspond to those produced by violent emotion. It is obvious that a person ridden by anxiety or fear will also be incapable of adapting himself to society.

Chapter III

From Effects to Causes

There is a word that we can, generally speaking, apply to the state of being ill at ease in company—and that word is "shyness." Other factors are also present, emotion, fear, inadaptability.

If shyness is only a symptom, the same goes for emotion and fear. So we must look for the causes which produce all these discomforts, these depressions, these fears, these attacks of sensitiveness and nervousness. Why these feelings of panic, of guilt, of being rejected by society, a society to which the sufferer wants to feel he belongs?

THE FEELING OF INFERIORITY

This is the most common of them all. It gives the shy person a vague feeling (sometimes amounting to a certainty) that he is *inferior* to others, and the impression (naturally) that others are better than he is. And even if, when he thinks about it objectively, he knows the opposite to be the case, there is nothing he can do. This impression of being inferior sweeps away reason and firmly digs itself in, defying all logic.

He feels humble, insignificant, despised. The symptoms of shyness reappear. The only difference is that shyness is an *effect* pure and simple, while the feeling of inferiority is a *cause.*

 It is only in comparatively recent years that this inferiority complex, as it is called, has been written about, but it is nothing new. It is just that until a fairly short time ago the sometimes frightening role it can play in human lives was not understood, or the fact that it could pave the way to failure for millions of people.

The removal of the feeling of inferiority is of paramount importance. It is a question of how we react to other people.

Is it abnormal to feel inferior?

It is *normal and natural for a child* to feel inferior. A child is small, extremely fragile and is plunged into a strange, mysterious world. The child collides with things and hurts itself, hears loud voices, looks up at monstrously large bodies, and has to discover a world that often seems hostile. But little by little the natural feeling of being inferior to everything develops in the child a desire to grow up, to do what its parents do and to imitate its elders. It is this feeling of inferiority that inspires the growing child to make up all manner of games in which it copies adults.

So what normally happens? The feeling of inferiority disappears *as the personality asserts itself.*

Thus, anything that hinders the young personality from asserting itself will encourage the feeling of inferiority to continue. And here we are talking about something that is vitally important for the future development of young lives! For things don't always turn out as they should ideally. Under the influence of environment, upbringing, religion, the feeling of inferiority can be imprinted in a child's mind as easily as an imprint in soft dough. This feeling will become a thorn in the flesh, morally speaking. Unless the situation changes, the thorn will remain embedded throughout adolescence. It will then leave a deep wound that will stay sensitive all through life, and will become a source of failure, fear and shyness. It will also set various defence mechanisms in motion—aggressiveness, for example.

A few typical cases

- There are parents who compare a child with a more gifted brother, or with a "genius" of a young cousin. There are elder brothers who always treat the youngest as a baby and as of no importance.

- There are teachers who humiliate a child in front of the whole class because he has little ability, is poor or has some physical defect. The child loses confidence in himself, feels humiliated and wants only to get his revenge. This is quite natural. After all, whose fault is it?
- There are parents who think it's a catastrophe that they have a daughter rather than a son—and don't trouble to hide their feelings.
- There are teachers who demand from a child more than he can give, although he is trying to do his very best.
- There are children who are given too early the sort of responsibilities that go with adulthood and are treated roughly. They then feel they are being exploited. And when they *compare* their lot with that of other children, they feel very keenly the inferiority of their condition.
- There are mothers and fathers (such cases are common and much more serious) who dominate first the child and then the adolescent. In this way they obstruct the development towards maturity and spark off hatred and rebellion. So it is natural that powerful feelings of inferiority and *guilt* should appear when the

child grows up, together with the impossibility of accomplishing any action requiring a properly developed personality.

Being appreciated

All the cases I have quoted turn on the eternal problem of *upbringing,* and I'll come back to this later. In the meantime, let us admit that the most powerful motive actuating many human being is the desire to be appreciated. But is this normal? People want to be appreciated in society, by their superiors and their subordinates. Men want to be appreciated by women, by their wives, their children. I repeat—is this normal? *Would these people need to feel appreciated if they didn't think they were inferior to others?*

Alder, the psychologist, has developed this-idea at some length. For him, mankind should be basically unselfish. Thinking of the general welfare should be as instinctive as breathing. Why then does a man feel ill at ease in the company of others? Because, says Adler, he feels a sense of inadequacy. This reduces his feeling of solidarity with others and each rebuff to the estimation that he has of himself reduces still further this feeling of solidarity with his fellow-men.

All that is well and good—but the question remains unanswered. *Will a normal man feel inferior to other people?* My answer is "no." A man who is balanced and has had the benefit of an upbringing that has developed his self-confidence, will be able to adapt himself to any circumstances in life. Now, to be ill at ease in company means not being able to adapt oneself to that company, but one can be certain that the balanced man will have the ability to enter into social life with complete ease.

Self-esteem

I am not speaking here of the "Number One every time" attitude, of which many people are guilty. I am referring to a psychological phenomenon which consists in feeling able to resolve the problems that come one's way, simply because one has confidence in oneself.

We know how important in social life is the estimation of oneself. And we also know that if this estimate falls sharply, it can cause serious difficulties—terrible shyness, for example. Then follow repeated failures, fear, sexual problems and unhappy marriages.

This want of self-esteem results when a person is faced by a problem which he is incapable of solving.

An example. You are with others and an excellent pianist plays a work of Mozart's beautifully. You, who are not an excellent pianist, listen in wonder. What happens to your opinion of yourself?

- If you are balanced, this opinion will not waver at all, nor will you experience any feeling of inferiority. HE is a pianist. YOU are not, and that's all there is to it.
- If you are psychologically unbalanced you will feel inferior for a number of possible reasons. Perhaps it will be because the OTHER man commands the rapt attention of his audience, or because he is so very confident, or because the women all look at him. You will feel inferior, and in your own eyes will become a nonentity. And this state of affairs will continue until you have a chance to shine in some sector where you have special knowledge or skill. In this way you will have redressed the balance, which will be a "compensation."

What determines your opinion of yourself?

It depends on two factors:

- *On how difficult the task is.* The difficulties vary considerably from one person to another. Perhaps it doesn't bother you at all if you have to speak in public, while for your shy neighbor this same action represents a torture greater than he can bear. At the same time, perhaps you start stammering pitifully as soon as a woman gives you a coy look, while another man wouldn't pay any attention. And so on.

- *On how mature the individual is.* You may well be physically mature while psychologically you have been held back for some reason or other-complexes, childhood memories, etc. Now, life demands of you a *degree of adaptability corresponding to your physical age!* So if your mental age does not correspond to your physical age, the adaptation will not be made. Every time this happens, you will go down in your own estimation.

How to recognize these feelings of inferiority?

It is a question, of course, of tracking down the *outward* signs. Because only a psychological analysis could diagnose *in depth* these feelings of inferiority. But be careful here! In many magazines you will find questionnaires to which you are told to answer "yes" or "no". And the heading will be something like this- *"Do you suffer from an inferiority complex?"* By all means get some fun out of it, but don't take it seriously! The depths of the human soul cannot be diagnosed in fifty printed questions!

So how, without probing these depths, can we recognize a person who is suffering from feelings o inferiority?

By examining:

- The way he holds his head.

- His body movements.
- His gestures.
- The way he speaks.
- The way he walks.

With many people, it is enough to observe their general bearing and the way they walk. Look at those people over there! You would think they were dragging along an invisible load. And notice their weary gestures and the curve of their shoulders. Unless, of course, they are "compensating" (see page 44). In that case, they will be strutting along, holding themselves unnaturally erect and making curt gestures, like short men who are compensating for their lack of stature.

And look at the way they walk. They hardly lift their feet. (Unless, of course, they are trying to assert themselves, in which case they will be marching like soldiers).

And the way they smile. It is forced, inept like everything else they do. It is hardly a smile: it is more of a grin. Then they put out a hand for you to shake: timidly at first, as if they fear you are going to refuse them yours. And when you extend your's, they grip it too tightly-as if they fear you are going to snatch it back.

Their gestures are awkward, clumsy, stiff. Slow

and lifeless or, on the contrary, much too quick. With a person suffering from a feeling of inferiority, the position of the hand can tell a lot. While he is talking, his fingers—though not the thumb or forefinger—will be drawn in as if he were hiding something in them.

You see such people in everyday life. They always seem to be on the watch. Since they suffer from a feeling of inferiority, they naturally try to protect themselves, almost to conceal themselves. It is as if they were forever in enemy territory. You can often see them in a café or a place of entertainment. They sit in a corner, close to the wall. Or in a cafe they take up a position where they can turn their backs on most of the other people. The same thing in a restaurant, because they can't stand being looked in the face, owing to their perpetual fear of being made fun of or despised. In a cinema or a theatre, they sit in the very back row.

Are they aware of all this? Nine times out of ten—no. All these defence mechanisms function unconsciously.

Too often we imagine that a person is suffering from a feeling of inferiority pure and simple. But this is not so. This feeling of inferiority is what must follow when we go down in our own estimation. So naturally it infects the whole personality and is echoed in every action. Of course, this is more noticeable in the social sphere. The fact that there are other people around aggravates the situation. However, even outside society the feeling of inferiority will by no means be absent. It smolders under the ashes, that's all.

That is why a feeling of inferiority (like shyness which is a symptom of it) manifests itself in *all* the actions of daily life. We always find that a strong feeling of this nature is present in neuroses, delinquency, drug-addiction and sexual perversions. Because the basis of all these vices or faults is a deep depression due to the sufferer having experienced a great blow to his self-esteem. At the same time, we always find too a desire to dominate (the mechanism of compensation).

I must tell you a little story recounted by Adler.

▯ Three children visit a zoo. They come to the lion's cage, and when looking at the king of beasts, these three children experiences the feeling of being inferior in strength, if not in dignity.

Since they feel inferior, they also feel rather daunted, being so weak in comparison with the animal. What are their reactions?

"I want to go home," whimpers the first child.

"Pooh!" says the second," I'm not a bit afraid!"

"Shall I spit in its face?" says the third scathingly.

Which is the least normal reaction? That of the third child. His inferiority has been "compensated." He played the hero. He became a little show-off—with whom many adults would do well to compare themselves from time to time!

Chapter IV

Escape!

How can we help ourselves to escape from this situation? Is it possible to be at our ease, neither timid nor aggressive, wherever we may happen to be? Can we, without having to go to a psychologist, eliminate shyness and an inferiority complex? Of course there are some cases which demand the help of a specialist but generally speaking, a person can overcome his shyness, at least as far as its main manifestations are concerned.

First of all, here are the basic principles which we must constantly keep in mind:

- The human being is at once material and spiritual, individual and social.
- To reform the character it is essential to *be aware* of the human condition and its responsibilities.
- To reform the character involves a diligent search for the factors that have produced shyness and feelings of inferiority.

It also means:

- Correcting our mistaken ideas, which means we must first know what these are.
- Sorting out what we really are from what we imagine we are— recognizing our true image and rejecting the idealized one.
- Understanding that character corresponds to the picture that a person has formed of himself—and that this picture influences *everything* he does, from the loftiest of thoughts to the smallest of gestures.
- Facing up to the obsession with self, its unreasonableness, its demands, false humility, pride, vanity and unconfessed fears.

All this demands a deal of courage. It is never pleasant finding out you are not what you think you are. Human beings have a tendency to deceive themselves, refusing to acknowledge anything that shows them up in a bad light. How many men want to "act big" if only to themselves! Why? *Because it saves them from confronting themselves as they really are.*

Thus it is essential

- To get to know ourselves better, to be honest with ourselves.
- To train ourselves to correct every day the

errors of judgment we make concerning ourselves.

- To achieve psychological maturity, a maturity which will enable us to adapt ourselves immediately to all circumstances, and therefore to any social occasion.

KNOW YOURSELF

It is impossible to eliminate shyness, fear or a feeling of inferiority without seeing ourselves as we really are. Shyness is only superficial— on the outside only. Shyness is a sort of "wrapping paper" which often contains a parcel that has nothing to do with this shyness! Moreover, it is useless to try to eliminate an effect without establishing the cause. That is obvious.

Here are some more important points:

- We should never look for the cause of a psychological trouble— timidity and inferiority, for example—in outward demeanor but rather in some *false inner attitude.*
- When this inner attitude is clearly understood, it becomes easier to eliminate the trouble.
- If we don't manage to eliminate it, we can be certain that this inner "block" will continue.

Let us remember that shyness in an indication of the character as a whole. It reveals what lies deep down, just as smoke betrays the existence of fire. It is no use battling against the smoke without putting out the fire. Thus, if we want to combat shyness, we must begin by exploring the character, from which the shyness derives.

If you want to conquer your shyness, you will have to ask yourself this question. *"What is my fundamental character really and truly like?"*

Generally speaking, we tend to find that:

- All shy people find it difficult to act. They are weak when it comes to action.
- All shy people are hesitant to get ahead, to fight and to win.
- All shy people are incapable of asserting themselves—except, in some cases, by aggressiveness and cynicism.

Is will-power the solution?

Quite definitely: NO. it is not will-power that is needed here. Will-power has never eliminated timidity. It is all too easy to say to the timid—"All you have to do is to use a little will-power!" It would be very easy, but would also be useless. It would be like asking them to battle against a strong current without being able to swim. What they must do is to learn to swim. Then there will be no need to push them into the water. Then will do that on their own.

Another question arises. Some people are *temperamentally* shy—the sentimental and the highly-strung, for instance. Can they uproot what has been planted in their biological nature? No! why should they try to do this anyway? No matter what the temperament is, great things can be accomplished. No matter what our temperament, we can all create and build something. So what must they do—these people who are timid by temperament? They must bring out the best in themselves. They must examine themselves and "purge" their characters of all objectionable elements. The sentimental person may remain shy, but he will then be able to act freely, without being held back by any internal "block" which has nothing to do with his being shy.

ISOLATION

All psychological miseries—shyness, inferiority complex and fear—are the direct consequence of a feeling of isolation, of loneliness.

The timid person who wants to correct this should bear constantly in mind:

- He feels isolated and cut off from society by his shyness, but tends to cast upon others the responsibility for his isolation, instead of blaming himself for it.

Is it always wrong for him to blame others? No. It is probable that there is something in his past that has destroyed, rapidly or by degrees, his self-confidence. It may have been the wrong sort of upbringing, or authoritarian parents. Perhaps his brothers and sisters were favored at his expense. Perhaps he has suffered from a feeling of religious or sexual guilt. And so on. There are thousands of possible causes.

However, the shy person must realize that:

- Whatever may be responsible for his shyness, it cannot be said that all humanity is at fault! If a field of corn contains a few weeds, it doesn't mean that the whole field is useless. If it is his upbringing that has made him timid, it doesn't mean that *all mankind* resembles those who brought him up. If his father was a tyrant, it doesn't follow that all men are like his father. This tendency to generalize is common among shy people, because they see in everyone the particular person who made them suffer.
- So they must look *to the present and not the past,* and say to themselves—*something in my past drove me to isolation, but that is all in the past, and I must now devote my attention to the present and to realize how absurd it is to let my past become*

a vicious circle, instead of trying to break away from it.

Stop living in a fool's paradise

Many shy people take a sort of pride in their isolation. They pretend it doesn't trouble them in the least and even congratulate themselves on their solitary state. They will say that—"Only the recluse is capable of rising above mediocrity" or" All the ills of this world stem from the fact that people live *en masse.*" Are they right? They would be, if they didn't suffer as result of it. But they do suffer from their isolation and everything they say shows that they are *trying to find a way of justifying themselves.* They live a solitary existence because they are incapable of adapting themselves to society but the sadness of such a life is there for all to see. It is obvious that a life outside the community is a life without love, and therefore no life at all.

So they must:

- Either persist in their isolation and accept the suffering it brings

or

- Force themselves to break out of it and return to the community.
- To do that, they must find out how to eliminate an attitude that has become a habit.

How to do this?

Or rather, what do they usually do? First of all they try to "force" themselves to change—and they have very limited success. When this method fails, as it does nine times out of ten, they appeal to reason. They try to tell themselves that the whole thing is "absurd" or "ridiculous" but once again without much success. The shyness and loneliness does not yield one inch. Then they commence to have a deeper insight into themselves. They discover, for instance, that they cannot stand criticism and that, if they shut themselves away, it is more from a fear of criticism than from shyness. Now they are making progress! They notice too, for instance, that they have a tremendous need to be appreciated, and that they cannot tolerate the smallest joke against themselves. And, in the end, they realize they want to avoid a society that is not struck with admiration for them.

We see then, from this example, that shyness is only a façade behind which hides something quite different! The person who succeeds in analyzing himself in this way has already taken a big step forward even if his falsely high opinion of himself suffers badly in the process.

Let's not fool ourselves

Take a man who is never a success in company.

What will he do? As I have said, he will probably blame his failure on to his shyness. But *above all* he will blame society for not understanding him, for not appreciating his true worth.

He will then say—"I shouldn't be so shy *if* I had a good car, *if* I had more money in my pocket, *if* that person who frightens me so much were out of my way, *if this, if* that ..."

So he admits his shyness up to a point but tries, nevertheless, to find "a good excuse" and looks for the culprit anywhere but the right place.

However, in his heart of hearts this man is often convinced that this point of view is just. He is sure that the removal of his shyness depends on all these "ifs." He doesn't realize that his shyness is a *general state* that affects his *whole* personality and that he is just as shy by himself as he would be if a hundred people were staring at him. With this difference—that he is not aware of his shyness when he is alone, whereas other people make him all too aware of it!

An example

Jean had to leave school at the age of seventeen because her father went bankrupt. She took a job but didn't like it, and became very bitter about her circumstances. As she came from a family that had always been rich, she felt humiliated at having to take a run-of-the-mill job like any other girl. She felt that her daily tasks were unworthy of her and her ability. So she began to complain about her ruined career, and gradually developed an inferiority complex, Little by little she became ashamed of her position and, when she was in company, she imagined that people thought of her as "a poor girl obliged to work because she has no money."

It goes without saying that Jean developed a deep hostility against society. "Both at work and outside, she said, "I'm a failure. But *if* only I'd been able to go on with my studies, I would be at peace with the world instead of hating it and being oppressed by it."

The moral of this story? Jean lacked inner strength there's no doubt about it. Of course, her circumstances were trying—but did the circumstances justify her behavior? No, not at all. Jean reacted as she did because she lacked real courage. She was incapable of adapting herself to a new situation, unpleasant as it may well have been. This lack of courage would have existed in her just the same even if she had been able to go on with her studies without a care in the world. As soon as the new situation arose, all this insecurity was let loose. *It wasn't the new situation which made Jean shy, but a lack of inner strength which made her unable to adapt herself. Shyness was only a symptom.*

TRAINING

Let us look now at the obstacles that the timid person has to face. If he tackles them firmly he will develop a calmness and ease that will enable him to get on and make real progress.

MOLEHILLS AND MOUNTAINS

The timid person is too easily hurt. The smallest attack—or faintest criticism—wounds him. Remember that his temperament inclines him to believe himself unwanted, misunderstood, misjudged!

Moreover, he tends to think that he alone is suffering, and should come to realize how mistaken he is. Once he knows that the streets are swarming with shy people, he will feel that his own shyness is less of a burden.

If you are shy, realize that susceptibility to criticism stems above all from the fact that you *do nothing about it!*

What should you do? You must train yourself to ask yourself—"Is this attack really directed at me? Is this really a very serious criticism? Or am I, in my emotional state, making a mountain out of a molehill? Did I worry all night over a merely trivial remark, or was there really something in what was said?"

So it is a question, then, of *not letting our emotions*

immediately get the better of us, but of consciously and coolly using our judgment. In this way, the shy person succeeds in rationalizing what he feels, and judging each occurrence of this kind at its true value. So, from the moment he begins sorting out the true from the false, there is every chance that he will leave his emotional state behind, instead of letting it lead him into long periods of brooding, which sometimes can go on for days and nights on end.

But remember. This training must not be undertaken *during* moments of stress—at least not to begin with. At these times the reasoning is blocked. So he must do these exercises in rational thinking *before or after* the unsettling incident, when he is calm and self-possessed.

Afterwards?

- Do everything possible to acquire a habit of serenity. We know that the shy person finds himself thrown off balance when confronted by situations which are new and therefore unusual.
- Forming a habit of serenity will enable the timid to overcome the introversion—and therefore the vulnerability—which shuts him away from other people. Furthermore, if this habit is acquired, he will be able, when he is

with" others" to concentrate on this habit instead of on himself.

- Anything can become habitual. The shy one should give up an hour every day to rehearsing, as it were. He should practise speaking slowly, gesturing easily, eating unhurriedly and calmly, and repeating over and over again the same serene behavior until it becomes automatic.

Train yourself to look at people!

Many shy people are afraid of others looking at them. If you are one of these, train yourself not to be. Don't turn your head away, but instead:

- Look the person who is talking to you straight in the eyes.
- Or direct your eyes to a point an inch or so above or below them. This will enable you to consider at your ease what the other person is saying and to weigh his words without being embarrassed by his gaze. Get into this habit. It's a basic principle in learning to look at people.
- When you have succeeded in controlling the way you look at people, train yourself to keep calm. Try to blink as little as possible. Try, little by little, to arrive at the stage where your thoughts and reactions produce no change in

your expression. If people criticize you, just listen to them as if you were taking careful note. If you receive compliments, show no sign of undue satisfaction. By training yourself every day—for about half-an-hour—you will find that you can acquire these extremely useful habits in no time at all.

RESIST THE TENDENCY TO "BROOD"

If you brood, a temporary wound can become a permanent injury. A shy person will turn over and over in his mind something that has upset him and end by convincing himself that he is incapable of getting on with people.

There are two remedies for this sort of brooding. One is learning to *act* at the right moment. The other is training oneself to *be calm*—again at the right time.

ACTION

All shy people think about themselves too much, as we know. They always consider themselves as life's *victims.* When they should do is to try to forget themselves and, in order to do this, they must turn their minds away from the things that provoke brooding.

First of all, the shy person should try to replace brooding *by thinking.* And while we are on this subject, this is what someone who used to suffer from shyness said to me:

It took me some time to realize that I enjoyed brooding. I liked feeling unhappy and making it obvious to other people. Why?Because I always hoped others would pity me—which would enable me to put the responsibility for my unhappiness on to them. Then I got wise to this, and it wasn't long before I had taken myself in hand. I was then on my guard against this brooding as soon as it started, and tried to replace it by reflection. I reasoned, weighed the pros and cons, and soon realized that there was nothing really to get so worried about. I also saw that, the more I brooded, the more tired I got—which in turn only encouraged the ideas to churn around and around in my head. I managed, day after day, to turn my passive state into an active one. In other words. to cut out brooding by conscious, intelligent thinking. This did me a tremendous amount of good and enabled me to see other people in a different light.

There is no doubt that all this would have been no better than a poultice on a wooden leg if the person in question had not trained himself consistently and deliberately. The shy person must grasp the opportunity as soon as it presents itself. The moment he starts to mope, he must stop dead and begin looking to see just how serious the wound is that he has received. At the same time he must make up his mind to act in precisely the same way whenever this situation occurs. In this way, he will soon replace brooding by action. As a result of repeatedly taking this course a habit will develop which will be strong enough to uproot the tendency to brood before it can grow.

SERENITY OF MIND

For many timid people—especially those who are highly-strung or sentimental—the banging of a door, the scratching of a pencil, or a sharp word are shocks which can be likened to stage-fright. They upset the nervous system, disturbing mental concentration as is the case with stage-fright, and bringing about a loss of self-control. Is it any help to say: "I don't want that to happen?" No! Will-power is not enough. *Progressive and sustained training* is the only remedy.

How can we cultivate serenity of mind? My advice to timid, emotional people is this:

- Select the sort of noise you hate most. For some, it will be blaring radio, for others, the creaking of a door and for others again, the boss's sharp, unpleasant vioce, and so on.
- Whenever these occurrences jar you, try to maintain—or quickly revert to—a composed face and mien.

- But don't overdo it! It is better that a certain amount of emotion should make its appearance than that you should unduly force yourself to suppress it.
- If it is possible to foresee the occurrence, prepare to compose yourself in advance. But don't consider the attempt has failed because complete calmness wasn't achieved. The important thing is to succeed in quelling the emotion as soon as possible after it has surged up in you.
- This training generally results in the person in question becoming immune to circumstances that he previously found insupportable. Not only do they produce no reaction in him, but the prospect of them does not make him the least bit anxious. The shy one who has submitted himself to this sort of training can therefore face without fear the prospect of having to meet people. Indeed, if someone speaks sharply to him, there is only a faint chance that he will get "stage-fright" and even if he has a moment of fear, he will have acquired sufficient self-mastery to throttle it immediately.

Other similar training methods

You should also practise controlling your other senses. Think of everything that is disagreeable to you as an ideal training ground. Don't run away from repulsive sights or unpleasant smells. For example, if someone gives you his hand and it is so clammy as to be repugnant, do not be in the least disturbed and treat this experience as another step in your training.

To sum up. Every victor over "jumpiness" is another step along the road to serenity of mind, something which is essential to the self-control that is a necessary part of social life.

AMBITION

Most shy people are fundamentally ambitious (especially) those who are highly-strung or sensitive). This ambition is part of their character.

But we find a contradiction here right away:

- The shy person is ambitious.
- In order to realize his ambition, he must assert himself.
- His shyness has made him profoundly unassertive.

What can be done about this contradiction?

Many shy people have very high ideals. They hide them deep down within themselves, cherish them, muse over them and consider how to realize them—one day. In the meantime, they remain unrealized. But sometimes they try to take action, but do it impulsively, without having reasoned, without having weighed the pros and cons, without having considered the snags and the chances of failure. They are like a sailor who sets sail without provisions or compass.

Obviously, obstacles soon present themselves. What does the shy person do? He gives up and he turns back. His inferiority complex comes into play and he decides he in nowhere near good enough to realize his ideals. He tells himself that it would need a strength that he *thinks* he doesn't possess. The attempt to achieve his ambition breaks down completely—until the next time he tries.

Can one train oneself to overcome this sort of inertia? Without a doubt—yes.

- The shy person tends to exaggerate his failures but he is not sufficiently aware of this. He must realize that, in his eyes, the failures always loom larger than the successes. He must recognize that to dwell upon his failures gives him an excuse to complain and to pass the responsibility for his discomfort on to society. This bolsters up his pride and his conviction that he is "different" from others.

- He must also realize that he always has an urge *to succeed the first time.* Why has he this urge? Quite simply because he feels *inferior.* So, he wants to make up for this inferiority by a *superiority,* which he would like to be *immediate and dazzling.* He wants—often without realizing it—to run before he can walk.
- He must fight these tendencies step by step. He must learn little by little how to get on with other people—to fight against his desire for isolation and, in order to do this, seek out friends who will not bully him and will never talk about his shyness. That is to say, friends with whom he can relax and be himself.
- He must learn to accept failure and criticism. He must learn that one must never run away from life because of fear of failure, and that failure can be the touchstone of success.
- He must watch his *pride* because it can very often be misplaced. He must acquire a sense of responsibility. Not the sort that say "I am guilty of this or that failing", but "I must learn to look to the future, instead of brooding over my past. I must throw myself wholeheartedly into things and seize opportunities whenever

they present themselves (after having considered them carefully), and I must also realize that when one thing has succeeded, other successes will automatically follow, and that it is the first steps that count."

- He must discover a *sense of purpose.* Shy people, as I have pointed out, are often intelligent and high-minded. So it goes without saying that they do not have to dig deep within themselves to discover this sense of purpose. They must let themselves be guided by reason and morally. Their secret, and often vaguely conceived, ideals will then have something solid to rest on, and the desire to do great things will be backed up by the power to do them.

Chapter V

Getting to Know Oneself...

As I have said again and again, shyness is only a symptom, and its causes must be tracked down to their source. I have also shown that a feeling of inferiority is often one of the causes of shyness.

But what causes feelings of inferiority?

Here we enter the "backroom" of the human character. We ask ourselves this question: can a man rid *himself* of these deep-seated inhibitions? Can he uproot them himself, without the help of a specialist?

In order to uproot them, he must first of all be able to *see* them clearly. But, supposing they lie at a subconscious level—how can he then become *consciously* aware of them? Are we asking the impossible?

I can't give a definite answer to this, sometimes it is possible, sometimes it isn't: but, in any case, we can get as far as analyzing our fear and sense of inferiority.

Concentrating on one aspect of a problem

This is what shy people do. There is, as I have already said, a definite technique in the art of deceiving oneself. It consists of concentrating on one aspect of a problem and then exaggerating its importance. One then comes to believe that everything else depends on it. One forgets that *the whole of one's life is in reality conditioned by the fundamental attitude of one's character.*

If someone is a victim of "complexes" he may very well keep telling himself: "I'm shy—but he will only be seeing a small fraction of the problem. Why? Because his "shyness" is only one aspect of his character even though it's the most obvious to him at the time.

It is easy to say, "I'm shy." Plenty of people are, and it's nothing to be ashamed of. But it is far less easy to recognize the other aspects of one's character because these may give us good cause to be far from pleased with ourselves.

The case of Paul T-

I tell this story because it could serve as a mirror to millions of shy people.

- Paul T-has an influential position in a large firm. He is much respected for his high qualities, for his intelligence and learning.

When people have a personal problem, they go to him. They admire him. Does this make Paul T-vain? It doesn't appear so. The situation seems quite natural to him.

Each morning there is a board meeting, which goes on for an hour, at which business is discussed. Paul T-begins to dread the very thought of attending these morning meetings. He says they make him terrible shy. This shyness bothers him to the point where he loses his appetite, is perpetually tired, lacks zest, suffers from headaches, sleeplessness, anxiety. At these daily meetings, the mere fact of saying yes while others were gazing at him numbs his brain, makes him go pale and feel faint. He longs "to get up, to clear out and get away from it all."

And Paul T-goes on to say: "It's really only these office meetings that affect me in this way. As soon as the meeting is over, most of my worries disappear."

One day—sensing that his nerves were going to pieces—Paul T-set about seriously "analyzing" his trouble. He bought books on psychology. He studied Freud. He enlisted the help of a professional psychologist.

And this is what the specialist told him:

"Rest assured there is something else behind this shyness of yours. It's like a scab hiding a deep festering wound. Firstly, you will have to see whether your shyness does stem extends to other occasions. Ask yourself this question; when do you feel happiest—or least unhappy?'

Clues

Paul T-set to work. First of all he discovered that:

- He was happiest of all when he was completely alone.
- Then when he was with his wife.
- Then came the office.
- Then, bottom of the list, at the dreaded morning meetings.

And the more Paul T-examined himself, the more he was convinced that this was the right order. And the more he became convinced of this, the less he understood. Why did the company of his wife, whom he loved, take second place?

Then he decided:

"My timidity is just a lot of nonsense. The fact is: I'm horribly afraid of being criticized or blamed. If I were really shy, a compliment would embarrass me, but the fact that people admire me gives me great pleasure. So, I'm afraid of criticism, even the most good-natured—but why?"

Why indeed?

He went on searching, and then went to see a new psychologist.

"If your fear of criticism is so terrible" this one said to him, "it is because you feel threatened. But by what?"

"I've no idea" replied Paul T-

"Think further" said the psychologist. "Is it not that you are afraid of being found to be less than perfect?"

"What do you mean?"

"What I say. You are probably scared of finding out that you're not perfect, and that all the admiration you have attracted so far is far from being a true reflection of what you are really like deep down."

Paul T-was furious, and left the psychologist's consulting room, banging the door behind him. How dare he question his superiority!

The trail gets thicker

But Paul T-was highly intelligent and started thinking. Why should he be so angry because a psychologist had asked him that question? Why was he furious about the idea that he might not be perfect? Didn't this anger prove that the psychologist had hit the nail right on the head first time?

Paul T-realized one thing: the fear that he

experienced when he was with others had always existed—but had increased during the last year. Why? He thought, and then suddenly remembered something his wife had said:

"Do you know what our friend Yvonne said to me? That there is something bogus about the high reputation you've got!"

Paul T-hadn't shown any reaction, but it had given him a nasty shock all the same. So, this Yvonne had dared to call his abilities in question! To suggest his intelligence and efficiency were no better than the next man's!

From that day on, Paul T's shyness was ten times worse. *Because someone had found out. Butt found out what?*

In fact, Yvonne had not put her finger on anything specific. But, as you might expect, her devilish feminine intuition had been at work and she had just "sensed" that all this "perfection" of Paul T-was a smokescreen, hiding something strange.

And was this true?

The other side of the picture

It was true. And Paul was forced (though how he suffered!) to admit it. He was highly intelligent, and well educated. He was utterly loyal, and was tolerant.

He was esteemed as a very kind person, and known for the way he considered others. In short, he seemed to be far removed from all the usual acknowledged human failings. And Paul T's fine qualities (*which in fact were genuine)* made him esteemed by all who saw him, as a paragon of all the virtues.

Who was Paul T-? I'll tell you—or rather, I'll tell you what he discovered about himself:

- Paul T-thought himself timid: and the thing he feared above all was criticism;
- He feared criticism because he did everything he could to appear perfect, in every sphere of his life.
- His intelligence and culture made him really seem perfect in the eyes of others.
- It was this seeming perfection that powerfully compensated for his intense feelings of inferiority.
- This inferiority complex forbade him to appear imperfect.
- His "shyness" had grown ten times worse since Yvonne's remark.
- He had told himself that if a woman could see through his "façade" of perfection, then anyone else could.

- From that moment he steeled himself, to do everything he could to buttress the fortress of his perfection. He was on his guard against anything that might show that he was a man just like other men.
- Worry gripped him because his inner security was only a pretence, and he needed other people's admiration in order to compensate for his feelings of inferiority.
- Even with his wife he experienced a terrible "shyness" which took the from of curt arrogance. Because his wife, who admired him tremendously, might also discover his weaknesses and at the same time she might cease to be as utterly devoted as she had been previously to a husband whom she had put on a pedestal.

Shyness recedes

When Paul T-had discovered all this, his shyness diminished considerably. This was understandable, because he had realized that *what he called his "shyness" didn't exist!* However, he was still very troubled. Why? Because he had stopped fooling himself and was beginning to see himself as he really was. He bravely set to work and learnt that a man attains full stature *from the moment he accepts himself as he is.* Little by little, he was able to relax when with his wife. He talked to her about his secret fears and anxieties. With her help, he analyzed himself. He soon realized that Yvonne's remark, frivolous as it may have been, had hit the target. *Because his whole life had been based on this delusion of perfection, which he had developed in order to obtain peace of mind and a defence against his feelings of inferiority.*

Whence did his feelings of inferiority derive?

In fact (as with many people) they derived from his childhood. In Paul T's case, authoritarian parents had obstructed all his efforts to attain a normal lively adolescence. When Paul rebelled and said "But how can I grow up properly if you never let me do anything on my own? How can I developed a personality?"—his father had replied "You don't need a personality as long as I'm here. "This of course was absurd, but that's how it was—and it is not surprising that he soon came to develop a feeling of humiliation and of inferiority to others. Wasn't it natural that he should rely on his keen intelligence to get on in life and to retrieve some of his self-assurance?

Thus he had built up his whole life on pretence until the day a woman by the name of Yvonne...

What happened then? He realized that his shyness

did not make sense and saw that, even at his age, he was still behaving as he had done with his parents.

He said to himself: "I'm no longer a child. I can't go on living in my unfortunate past. My own qualities are real enough. Why should I be behaving as if I were still under my parents' rule?"

Which, for Paul, was an immense step towards ridding himself of his "shyness."

CAUSES

Behind all true shyness there is always "something else" concealed. Does this always apply? Yes. And what are the main causes of shyness?

SOCIETY AND ITS LAWS

Society is rather like the Loch Ness Monster. Everyone talks about it, but no one ever sees it. It's a bit like the mythical hydra: invisible, it stretches out hundreds of tentacles in all directions.

Society lays its hands on us from a very early age. It immediately tries to fashion us by imposing its laws and shaping us in its image.

What image? The family, school, religious and sexual moulds. From childhood onwards, we are caught up in a web of laws, obligations, rules, restrictions and taboos. We are seized in a vice which prevents us from acting according to our instincts and our needs. It is obviously right that this should be so, for otherwise a human being would soon reach a state of personal anarchy within a codified society. And so it is no time at all before the child hears *You can do this because it's good"*(which really means it's allowed) or *"You can't do that because it's bad"* (which really means that society has decided against it).

If the child rebels against society, something will soon be done about putting him on the "right path. "Very often the child has no understanding of what it's all about, but obeys out of fear of the consequences—harsh words, or even blows. And *immediately* he feels frustrated and belittled.

So we see that many things in life can bring about a feeling of inferiority, and therefore shyness and an inability to adapt socially. Does this depend on circumstances? Yes, obviously, to a certain extent, but it depends above all, as I have said, on the person's *inner* reaction to these circumstances. Which is why, in the same situation, one person will become timid, another will assume a bullying manner, while a third will remain calm and unmoved.

What are the great social restrictions?

There are three of them. But, like the three musketeers, they do enough damage for ten.

They are:

- Family and school life.
- Religion when it is misunderstood or misapplied.
- Sex when it is mistaught or misunderstood.

You can be certain that these three factors are great potential breeding-grounds for "shyness" and that nine inferiority complexes out of ten can be traced back to one of them, or to a mixture of them.

FAMILY AND SCHOOL LIFE

This, in spite of the best intentions in the world, is often one of the main factors behind a feeling of inferiority.

A child often occupies an important place in the family. It is obvious that, from the beginning of its life, a child will react to its immediate surroundings and therefore to its family environment. He will quickly develop his "way of life," which will be implanted (often permanently) in his brand-new brain.

Thus the fact of being the eldest or youngest child is of great importance. Being the eldest or the youngest represents a "situation." The child will react to this situation by behaving in this or that way. This reaction depends on the child, of course, but also on the family environment. One can see that it all depends on whether this environment is serene, whether it is intelligent, whether it is well-to-do, and so on.

What does an eldest child often do? From the moment the younger brother or sister is born, he (or she) loses the privileged position to which he has become accustomed—that of the only child, pampered and petted. How does he react? Often by becoming rather bossy. By protecting the younger brother or sister, he "compensates" for its sense of inferiority. In this way he tries to get back its position as the first of the family—and at the same time derives satisfaction from lording it over the younger child, which he takes under his wing. If this situation goes on, the elder child will become ambitious and will feel the desire to be number one in everything.

The youngest child will often be petted and protected, both by his (or her) parents and by his brothers and sisters. But nine times out of ten, he will reject (often subconsciously) this mollycoddling, especially when he gets a bit older. He will become a rebel—and later on, a revolutionary. He will become a shy person seeking to assert himself and the result will be a social misfit.

There are hundreds of possible variations, of course. But all I wish to stress is that our childhood experiences *always* have a powerful influence over our later lives.

A typical example...

It is that of a boy growing up among sisters older than himself. What happens? The boy is always surrounded by girls, all older and therefore "superior" to him. So he will soon start thinking subconsciously that all members of the female sex are stronger than himself. This is natural, because all the women around him are in fact stronger than he is—mother, sisters, aunts, his mother's and sister's friends. Thus the boy is bound to have feelings of inferiority to the opposite sex. If the situation doesn't right itself we shall see him, when he grows up, running away from women—and eventually marrying a "strong" woman, more energetic than he, who will dominate him—and by whom he will willingly let himself be dominated. The result will be a shy, timid, weak man, a society misfit.

Another typical case

Here is the commonest sort of case and the one most responsible for social misfits. It is that of the boy brought up by his mother. Either:

- His mother is a widow.
- She has a weak husband who is therefore of no importance.

One can predict that eight times out of ten, the boy will reach maturity with a strong inferiority complex.

It is easy to understand why:

- The mother, who morally has to stand alone, pampers and protects her little boy.
- At a very early age, the boy becomes tied to her apron strings. This dependence he enjoys. For him it means security, tenderness and affection.
- As he gets older, he will want little by little to escape from the nest and try out his own wings. His masculine personality will show itself with the advent of puberty, and he will then want to fend for himself.
- His mother will go on pampering him, often without realizing what is happening.
- The boy would like to rebel against his mother and break through the barriers that prevent his becoming a man.
- But he can't rebel because his mother is kindness itself.
- Bit by bit, the boy loses his "manliness."

A very important point!

- The boy is troubled by a nagging worry over his desire to rebel against his mother.
- But as his mother is almost sacred, a paragon of goodness against whom he is morally

forbidden to rebel, the boy experiences a profound sense of guilt.

- As he feels guilty towards his mother, he puts everything he has into playing his "little boy" role. Why? Because (1) this pleases his mother and (2) it enables him to retain his mother's love—and therefore no longer to feel guilty.

The result

The boy makes a mess of his life. He leaves the road that could lead him to true manhood and to his place in society and becomes a perfect example of the social misfit. He feels ill at ease, guilty, inferior, effeminate and shy. He is afraid of women, unless his fear turns into scorn or hatred.

It is very difficult for a mother to love without pampering. But the price to be paid is the boy's future mental well-being, beginning with his sexual life, about which I will say word later.

Upbringing and shyness

The root cause of a lot of shyness can be traced to parents and teachers who are too strict or who don't understand the mentality of children.

These people imagine:

- That a little boy is a man in miniature.
- That a little girl is a smaller edition of a woman.

Obviously, they are wrong. They imagine that the actions of a child have the same moral implications as those of an adult. They do not know that many things a child does have no importance. If a little boy "pinches" a coin or two, it doesn't mean he is headed straight for prison! So in dealing with children we must take full account of their true nature, and not apply adult principles to them.

Many inferiority complexes and social misfits result from these errors. The child does something "immoral"—theft, masturbation, lies and such. What do some people do? They immediately start talking about sin, evil, the devil, eternal punishment, and heaven knows what else! They act in such a way that the child thinks of his "sin" as having an importance far beyond its desserts.

Thus the child feels branded. I have known fathers who, having heard that their child has stolen something, have said in effect: "The devil saw you! And everyone—all your friends, all your teachers—know about it because it's written on your face! But no one will say anything about it to you, because they're ashamed of what you've done!"—and other such stupid things.

Instead of reassuring, understanding and helping the child, these people are ruining him. This kind of treatment can warp his outlook and do him permanent damage. He may well carry a sense of shame wherever he goes. When he reaches adulthood, he may feel an outcast and rejected by others. Many adolescents shun other people like the plague, simply because of this sense of shame that had been inculcated in them. And, when they grow to maturity, they will suffer from a crushing feeling of inferiority! They will say "I'm shy" without knowing why they are shy or that it is the acts of others that have made them so.

Giving security

A child needs, above all, to feel secure. If strict parents can do harm, those who are over-anxious can do still more. Many people are timid because they have been brought up in an atmosphere of anxiety. They have been in the hands of parents or teachers who themselves were timid and pessimistic in their outlook. In all good faith, these adults have spoilt the liveliest and healthiest of children. As they themselves are unbalanced, they pass on this condition to the children they bring up. So what does the child do? It becomes a sad, melancholy sort of adult who thinks life is hardly worth living. All its natural high spirits are dried up—and once more we have someone saying "I'm shy."

WHEN RELIGION IS MISUNDERSTOOD

Too much religious instruction is based on an anxious dread of doing wrong, and on notions of rewards and punishments, both in this life and the next.

One thing stands out. Far too many parents paint God and the Devil as if they were ever-present bogeymen. Just as if they were saying, "If you're not good, the policeman will come and take you away. "To quote Voltaire: "If God created Man in His image, Man has returned the compliment!" But in trying to teach morals, we must not abase God to the level of a Zeus armed with Neptune's trident. We need only imagine the state of mind of a child or adolescent having to face such an image of God when he feels guilty of some "sin" (lying, masturbation, etc.)!

I knew a mother who said to her thirteen-year-old son—a boy who was sensitive and emotional: "*You hear the wind in the trees? That is the souls of the damned who moan every time you commit a sin!*" I agree that these words were profoundly stupid. Now, this boy used to practice self-abuse. He had always heard sex talked about as if it were something secret and shameful, and "the solitary vice" as the most terrible sin there was. Never any explanation, never a reasoned warning. The result? At the age of sixteen, puberty increased the urge to masturbate (although he didn't dare admit the habit to anyone). For a year, the boy lived in a torment of fear—though he told no one about it because that would have meant telling the rest too. Further result? At the age of seventeen, he started having hallucinations, mixed with obsessions of guilt. At nineteen, the young man attempted suicide.

Is this an extreme case? *In the form it took—perhaps. But basically, no.* A narrow view of religion always produces powerful feelings of guilt.

Guilt and society

If a child (or an adolescent) has been brought up in an atmosphere of guilt, how can he possibly be at ease with others?

He will imagine himself" different from others." He will have the feeling that he is impure or perhaps branded. *He will feel rejected by society.* It will be fatal if he develops feelings of inferiority and a grudge against society. As an adult he will be shy and will feel guilty towards the whole of society, because this guilt will become *part and parcel* of his life.

Religion properly understood

Properly understood, religion should develop in us the courage to see ourselves as we are. It should inspire love, a pride in ourselves, for a start, rather than shame for ourselves. Religion should engender in us serenity and confidence, thus enabling us to surmount the difficulties of our private lives.

To get back to the question of upbringing. If a parent or teacher goes in fear of a terrible avenging God, he can never do other than pass on these fears to the children in his care.

This alone lies at the basis of millions of inferiority complexes.

SEX AND TIMIDITY

There is too often a tendency to think of sex as such a private affair that there is something shameful about it. In schools, more importance is so often attached to learning the cities of Europe by heart rather than to the rules of community living.

What has the community to do with sex? The great mistake we make in talking about sex is to consider the individual as separate from society. We imagine that sex life is a thing apart in an individual. And that the community is supremely uninterested in the sex life of its individuals—as long as they don't cause a scandal.

Shyness often has a sexual basis

Our sexual behavior is bound up with love (or it

should be). It is then a part of our social behavior which involves a great responsibility. *But who is concerned about the sex life of human beings?* Generally speaking, no one. Neither parents, nor teachers, nor doctors. Films are shown of "shameful disease." Thus we learn about sex in its lowest form. We study the mire before being shown the light. No one corrects these impressions by saying that real sex is something quite different!

Who hasn't seen good-looking and perfectly virile men go as pale as little boys when a woman looks at them? So many men, moreover, show themselves to be perfectly virile in the way they attack their daily tasks except in one respect—their attitude to women. Why this partial virility? Why this particular timidity? Once again, it's a question of upbringing.

The day when teachers and parents themselves succeed in throwing off sexual inhibitions, the day when they manage to think of sex with the same objectivity as they do other aspects of human nature—that day they will have taken an immense step forward which will enable a mass of men and women to adapt themselves to social life and get rid of their "shyness.

Has shyness always a sexual basis?

No, of course not! As I said, shyness is a symptom

which affects the whole personality. Shyness follows in the wake of an inferiority complex and affects *every* sphere of life. But in many of these spheres, we find the phenomenon of *compensation* (see page 45). The human being is then *obliged to pretend he is courageous.* This succeeds sometimes, and enables a man to live a more or less adapted social life. But nevertheless we can be sure that in the company of women his shyness will be as profound as ever. For this is the most difficult type of shyness to overcome because it stems from the taboos that surround sex.

When should a child be told?

At the age of four or five, a child asks many questions—and some of these questions *seem* to have a connection with sex. Now, a parent should know that a child's curiosity has nothing to do with sexual curiosity. If a child asks "where do babies come from?" it is very silly to blush. To say "You're too young—you'll find out about that later on" is also silly. It's enough to say, in perfectly good faith, that "a mother carries her baby under her heart"—and the child will be satisfied. You will have given him a clear, objective answer to a question which, for him, concerns only one of the many things he is curious about.

At the age of ten, it all begins again. The child

again starts asking questions that many parents and teachers find disconcerting. At this stage it becomes dangerous to deceive! We can be quite sure that the child will already have a keen sense of reality. So what should we do? Tell him the truth, quite simply and with sincerity. But here *everything depends on what sort of relationship exists between parents and children,* and on intelligence and tact, both of which must be used to the full. During this period of adolescence, the human being—and especially the boy— is disturbed and troubled by the physical and mental changes that are taking place in him. The emotion they produce is very strong. The adolescent finds himself confronted by mysterious forces that are awakening within him. *And this is the time when he should be able to feel he has the support and help of his elders.* And this help must be clear, precise, objective and candid. We are too often unaware that, for many adolescents, puberty takes the form of mental struggle that has a sexual basis. Is it not clear that aid from understanding adults can then be of enormous importance, both for the adolescent boy's future relations with women and for his future as a member of society?

SUMMING UP

If you have read all I have written so far, you will be persuaded of one thing—that many human beings have deeply-rooted feelings of inferiority, with all the accompanying symptoms.

You should know also that such people react in four ways:

- They hesitate.
- They run away.
- They hide themselves.

Then comes the painful depression. They feel defenceless and unhappy. They become timid and anti-social.

Or else:

- They become aggressive, resentful, hostile and vindictive. The strength of the aggressiveness is in proportion to the depth of the initial depression. They are on the attack the whole time, *but the attack is only a defence.*

But there is another form of behavior which is very common and shows itself in mild bouts of depression and shyness. The person assumes a composed expression and manner. He uses cunning in order to hide his shyness. He *wants to believe* he is strong. But since, deep down he doesn't believe this, he uses every possible means to make others do so.

Making a new start

Shyness stems from previous circumstances which

have no relation to the shy person's *present* situation. That is obvious. This basic characteristic is that he has *not developed properly*—and so he doesn't adapt himself to circumstances in the normal way. Moreover, the frequent efforts he has made to overcome his shyness have over-worked his nervous system. He makes a mess of something; he is ill-adapted to some circumstance or other. The first failure then leads to a second, similar to the first. At this stage, the situation need not be very serious. The shyness could be corrected by the right family environment or by understanding teachers.

Unfortunately, these initial failures are often followed by total silence. And, like an infection that spreads, a dread of failure affects everything he does. Fear sets in and with it an emotional stage that goes from bad to worse. So he retreats behind a glass wall. From this protection he looks out fearfully at what *the others* are doing, but is unable to join in with them (even if he imagines he is doing so, as in the case of the shy person who covers up by being aggressive).

Chapter VI

Treatment for Shyness

I spoke earlier of certain kinds of training that can be undertaken. But I also said that this training is only a preparatory stage in the job of eliminating shyness.

I am often asked *whether shyness is really curable.* And my reply is *"Yes, a hundred times, yes! As long as it is attacked at source and pulled out by the roots."*

One must realize that shyness—whether it takes the form of depression or aggressiveness—is an illness, not only because it is the symptom of a subconscious weakness, but also because it is the sum total of a number of abnormal reflex actions.

PHYSICAL TREATMENT

This consists above all in conquering *hyper-emotion* (see page 51). A doctor will have to be consulted if it is a case of deep-rooted hyper-emotion—for this sort of weakness can in itself give an impression of excessive timidity. Why? Because the person then reacts explosively to the most ordinary occurrence.

A highly emotional state can exist from birth, and then it is a matter of a person being *constitutionally emotional.*

On the other hand, hyper-emotion can be brought on by:

- Serious nervous disorders (brain upsets or perhaps great emotional shock).
- A generally run-down condition (weakness after an illness, under-nourishment, fatigue).
- Intoxication (alcohol or even tobacco, coffee or tea).
- Biological changes (puberty, menstruation or perhaps the menopause).

What will the doctor do? He will generally prescribe barbiturates in small doses or other sedatives.

Carefully induced relaxation, rest and the right sort of medical care and attention—these are all part of the treatment designed to help the over-emotional person to acquire a balanced outlook and to regain self-control.

PSYCHOLOGICAL TREATMENT

This can be done either:

- By self-treatment, or
- By specialist treatment by a psychiatrist.

Curing oneself

Once more I must stress, if this training is relatively easy to begin with, *complete self-cure is difficult and demands great courage and a deal of clear thinking*. Self-cure requires that one sees right down into oneself and is able to face boldly the inevitable pain and distress.

What is a shy person? He is one who has undergone emotional upsets. *But nine times out of ten, these upsets are pushed back into the subconscious.* Why? Because at the time they occurred they were too painful to face consciously. One can understand that, if he succeeds in bringing them to the surface, this proves painful also!

Nine times out of ten, a shy person has had to find some defence mechanism in order to combat the circumstances he cannot tolerate. (This was the case with Paul T-who "defended" himself by putting up a façade of perfection). He is often one who has built his life on shaky foundations, but without realizing it. *He can have been educated, got married, had children and brought them up while believing himself all the time to be quite a different sort of person from what he really is.*

If there is to be a cure for shyness, a thorough examination of the patient's inner life is essential.

Distress during self-analysis

Ill or well, all experience this. For everyone must be distressed when he has to judge himself. How can he fail to be, when he realizes that he hasn't so much to be proud of as he liked to think?

Let us take the case of a man who, at the age of forty, becomes profoundly aware of not being the person he thought he was. He has imagined himself to be a model of goodness and rectitude, but discovers that these imagined qualities are only a mask by means of which he has unconsciously *compensated* for his strong sense of inferiority and that, in reality, he is malicious, vindictive or selfish.

- Take a business manager. He believes himself intelligent, indomitable, dynamic, virile. But he discovers that he is only a "little boy" who is not at all manly, thanks (if that's the word) to the upbringing he had. He also discovers that his dynamism, and his crisp way of giving orders, are only compensations for the fear there is inside him.
- And let us take a mother with a twenty-year-old son, who realizes that she has done everything in her power to stop her son from developing into a young man because she wanted to keep him for herself as long as possible.

Can you imagine the anguish that such discoveries must cause?

But this anguish is essential and represents the first great stride towards real self-knowledge and a complete recovery.

It needs courage? Indeed it does.

However...

It is essential to be able to see clearly how and where the shyness originated. We must trace it back to its source, or we can accomplish nothing. It's not a question of pinning the responsibility for it on to someone or something at all costs, nor of wringing our hands in despair. What we have to do is to search through our past and find when and where we took a wrong turning.

First of all, the shy person will have to go back to his childhood. *He will have to set to work to analyse his past.* How was he brought up? What was his father like? And his mother? Was he an only child? Was he the youngest or the eldest of the family?

Starting from there, he will soon have a number of important clues which will set him on the track. He will have to search out the cross-roads in his life—the moment when he had to set up a "defence mechanism" which stood in the way of his leading a normal life.

You wish to examine yourself? You will have to look carefully at all the little circumstances of your daily life. You must analyse your reactions to the people you meet. These will give you an opportunity to get to know this strange being who lives inside you, who goes everywhere with you, and whose face you don't know. *But it is this person who leads you wherever he wants to!*

I have said that this takes plenty of courage. Tenacity too. It is not in just a week that we can assemble all the facts about ourselves. We have to work conscientiously, admitting our fears and shames when we uncover them. We must not allow ourselves to "cover up" something because it does not correspond to the image that we have of ourselves!

Above all, we must not be afraid. Let us imagine someone who wants to be psycho-analysed and the psycho-analyst says to him "All right, come and see me whenever you like." What will happen? *He will go as long as the psycho-analyst does not attack the image he has of himself.* But as soon as the specialist touches the wound inside him, as soon as he starts to investigate it, then the patient's escape mechanism will start working. Why? *Because he'll be afraid of coming face to face with himself.*

It is the same when, on our own, we look into ourselves. It is when we despise ourselves and feel that we are contemptible *that the most constructive work can be done.* It is then that we see ourselves as we are, that we become genuine, authentic human beings. Congratulations to those who get this far!

An example of self-training

How should a man who is afflicted with this shyness set about analysing himself? He must tell himself, in the first place, that his shyness is only a symptom. No good doctor, for example, would treat a heart complaint in isolation. On the contrary, he would consider it in relation to the whole organism.

Suppose then that the "shy" person notices he is tongue-tied during conversation with friends. He will have to find out why. Supposing he finds that: "I'm tongue-tied because I'm afraid they will criticize me or make fun of me."

What will he do then? He will say to himself "I'm frightened when I'm in company. I feel paralysed. Yet this fear has no basis in any real danger, so my fear is greaten than my desire to be popular. My fear is stronger than my desire to make a good impression."

He is already on the brink of discovering something important. What he will often find is this: "I want to make not only a good impression, but a perfect one. why? Because that would compensate for my inferiority complex. So it is natural that I should be afraid to speak, because if they criticize or contradict me, it will mean that I am not perfect. And I could not face that because it would plunge me back into my inferiority complex" (see the case of Paul T again, page 96).

And then...

At this point, he will have taken a big step towards understanding his problems. He will then have to check up on the other aspects of his life. He will analyse his relations with women. Why is he so timid when he is with them? Is he afraid they will discover his failings? What failings? Sexual failings? And, if that is the case, isn't because he wants to be above all criticism in this matter too?

Once on the right track, he will go forward. He will look to see where his difficulties in adapting himself to life originate. What were his parents like? Demanding? Tyrannical? Did *they* make him feel inferior? And in what way? By making him aware of his weaknesses, or by molly-coddling him? Had he violent feelings of rebellion against his parents? Did he feel guilty about this? Did he practise masturbation? If so, did he feel guilty about it?

Be careful! He should remind himself that all these things that he discovers about himself are *closely connected.* Not one of them is isolated from another.

So he will also need to see how they all link up. *Again be careful!* One of the great difficulties about self-analysis is the resistance that one meets, as I have already pointed out. When someone approaches one of the taboo subjects, he will *always* react emotionally. It may be fear, it may be anger. This is natural, since the taboo represents forbidden territory! If, for example, a young man suddenly realizes that there are moments when he hates his mother (because she dominates him, perhaps) he will be horrified and will tend to hide from himself the fact that these moments exist, because he cannot face them. The shy person who analyses himself will have to get used to looking *all* the feelings he experiences straight in the face, so that he can consider them as objectively as he does the vagaries of the weather.

In any case, the shy person who sets out systematically to discover his true personality, has every chance of being very successful. If shyness stems from subconscious wounds, it will disappear with the awakening of conscious awareness in the person who has suffered those wounds.

Help is sometimes necessary

To cure oneself it is necessary to look deep down into oneself. So many of us look "obliquely" at ourselves, going round and round in circles, and failing in everything we undertake.

Such people dwell on their failure, start the same thing all over again, time after time, without asking themselves why they have failed and what means they should adopt to prevent another failure. They go back into the same battle with the same weapons, which is absurd. They fight (always employing the same methods) without asking themselves whether what they are doing is expedient, whether they have got the right slant on it, or whether they are sufficiently well armed.

These people should seek the help of a psychiatrist. Probing our deepest instincts is not something we can all do, and there are certain behind-the scene adjustments that only a specialist can undertake, by using special techniques (psycho-analysis, for instance).

The psychiatrist can be likened to a gunnery expert who shows the recruit how best to aim the weapon. He teaches the calculation of the correct angles, and helps the patient to see those angles as they really are (and not as his unreal shy self sees them).

The psychiatrist knows just how far some people, going against their real selves, are capable of doing the very opposite of what they should in order to make a success of their lives. Innumerable factors can play their part in making a man act in such a way as to impede his own psychological development. He might, for example, make a bad choice of a partner in marriage and tie himself to a way of life that runs counter to what he really wants. And, if I choose this example, it is because it is as obvious as it is common—and because nine times out of ten a psychological failure lies at the root of it.

Timidity begets failure. There are some fathers who, without knowing it, do everything they can to make their homes unpleasant. There are business men who enter on jobs which are inconsistent with their real talents. Moreover, psychological failure can take the form of an illness which the person in question not merely contracts but actually encourages. It is difficult to believe that a man can be capable of forging, subconsciously, the weapons of his own destruction!

The psychiatrist will sometimes step in and lead his patient back on to the right path. He will track down former mistakes and the sources from which they derived, all this with the fullest co-operation of the "shy" person.

The psychiatrist will often meet shy people who say they have been cured by "suggestion" and add that "It's better to be cured by this way than not at all." Now these people make a great mistake. "Suggestion" has no place in the treatment of shyness.

The reason why it attracts so many people is that it represents an excellent method of escaping responsibility and above all, the unpleasant necessity of seeing oneself as one really is. Likewise, there are many people who are obsessed by hypnosis, and ask the psychiatrist to use this "method" to cure them. Now, suggestion and hypnosis would be like "poultices on a wooden leg." These methods would take a person back to the point where he started instead of bringing him safe and sound to the opposite shore. It goes without saying that treatment by suggestion only scratches the surface of the problem instead of penetrating to the heart of it.

Instead, the psychiatrist will try to restore the shy one to mastery of himself, by convincing him that he is not just the plaything of circumstances.

Little by little, the shy person must emerge from his shell and be *capable* of asserting himself. He will find that to do this does not call for superhuman efforts, but simply for the exercise of a controlled and balanced will-power.

In fact, the timid person will re-mould himself by learning to look about himself, and by throwing himself into what is going on outside him. Not because the psychiatrist will force him to do this, but because it will happen automatically as soon as other people cease to be bogeys from whom he runs in terror.

The specialist will thus teach his patient to say "yes" to life. But this "yes" cannot be elicited by shallow or superficial methods.

It's a question of digging deep, of penetrating the subconscious, and especially of reaching the stage where the patient can break down his own resistances.

The psychiatrist searches, above all, for what will enable his patient to attain *maturity*. And since the shy person's path to maturity is blocked" somewhere, it is the specialist's job to open it up again. It is therefore a question of the closest collaboration, whereby the timid person will become a new man, able to adapt himself easily to all circumstances, and a free man for the first time in his life.

What you should avoid

If you are shy, keep the following comparisons constantly in mind. Every day look at the left-hand page and then at the appropriate training exercises on the right-hand page. It is going to take more than a day to achieve results but, if you want to cure yourself, you will find these points

- Taking matters of little consequence to heart
- Acting on the spur of the moment
- Jumping at the slightest noise
- Getting quickly upset or offended
- Getting angry easily
- Getting emotional
- Changing rapidly from elation to dejection
- Judging everything with your heart
- Impatience
- A craving for sympathy

- Being slow in getting down to work
- Trying to do too many things at once
- Working merely because you feel you ought to
- Taking a superficial view of everything

What you should aim at

Extremely useful. The right-hand page, in fact, lists the main characteristics of the balanced man, whom you wish to become and whom you will become if you take your training really seriously.

- Taking only serious matters seriously
- Acting only after calm reflection
- Self-control under all circumstances
- Realizing that the other person probably meant no harm
- Control your temper at all times
- Be composed and calm always
- Maintain an even temperament
- Judging with your head
- Cultivate serenity and patience
- Stand on your own feet
- Act promptly and with decision
- Tackle jobs one at a time, and finish them
- Treat your work as a pleasure
- Look always for the underlying causes.

A little glossary

ANXIETY. A vague feeling of imminent and indefinable danger. This stage of tension is often accompanied by a heightened imagination which magnifies and dramatizes every problem.

CHARACTER. The inherent nature of a man, governing the way in which he generally reacts to the circumstances of life.

COMPLEX. The body of suppressed tendencies and emotions hidden in a man's unconscious, producing involuntary reactions against which his will is powerless.

DEPRERSSION. A feeling of gloom, a lowering of the spirits, transient or lasting. It is a condition of the nerves whose effects can be physical as well as psychological.

EMOTION. An excitement or agitation of mind and body. Under normal conditions, it will be in proportion to the stimulus which produced it. If it is exaggerated, it becomes hyper-emotion.

GUILT. A feeling which gives a person the impression that it is usually he that is at fault. It often causes great distress and can even induce a subconscious urge for punishment.

TEMPERAMENT. The ways in which a man's character expresses itself, according to his physical organization and his mental outlook.